FRESHER PRESSURE

A GUIDE TO UNIVERSITY

MADELINE CASTREY

First Published in 2020 by Blossom Spring Publishing

Fresher Pressure: A Guide To University

© 2020 Madeline Castrey

ISBN 978-1-8380982-2-3

E: admin@blossomspringpublishing.com

W: www.blossomspringpublishing.com

I would like to thank my Mum, Jacqueline for her endless support, love and encouragement.

I would also like to thank the wonderful Ellysia Manuel for her amazing designs/doodles and awesome talent! See more of Ellysia's work at: www.ellysiabellemanuel.com / Instagram - @ellysia.belle.designs

Lastly, I would like to thank YOU. If you're reading this book, you're courageously embarking upon an exciting and challenging journey – and I'm sure that whatever you learn will help you make the world a better place for many years to come.

CONTENTS

INTRODUCTION

Hi there! My name is Madeline, and I'm so excited to help you embark upon your university journey! At the time of writing this book, I am both a university student and staff member. I'm currently studying for my PhD in music at The University of Westminster at the same time as lecturing undergraduate students at The London College of Music. I love being on both sides of the lectern (if that analogy makes any sense!) University is such an important and unique journey, and it can be all too easy to lose sight of just how special this experience is once you settle into the responsibility of a job. In this book, I'll draw on some of my own experiences both as a student and a lecturer to help you navigate some of the hurdles that you might face over the course of your studies. Reading this book in advance of your first year might help you better prepare for the challenges you might face, or you may want to go through the chapters in "real time", so I can be the voice in your corner as you navigate your encounters!

Contrary to my job title, I'm not here to lecture you! Instead, think of me as a friend who might be able to help you through some of the trickier times, and who will also be celebrating your triumphs with you and cheering you on when you accomplish the success that I'm sure you'll achieve!

The fact is, each and every one of us are learning every day, and by the time your university journey comes to an end, you'll probably have enough experiences to fill a book of your own. For now though, I hope my own experiences and advice can provide you with some friendly, encouraging support as you start of the most wonderful journey that is university!

IS UNIVERSITY RIGHT FOR YOU?

If the time has come to consider whether university is right for you, a maHOOSIVE well done is in order! You've got through junior school exams, GCSEs and are now just a few A levels away from the next big part of your life. You're about to start a whole new chapter that isn't just about the education – it's about that other word "adulting." Living on your own, managing your money, coming and going as you please, all spring to mind when you think about that word, and while some people might tell you "you're not ready for all that" – I'm here to tell you that you are. By getting to this point in your life, you have already proven that you're able to handle the pressure of exams, and balance meeting up with your friends with revision and study. You'll already have the fundamentals of time management, prioritisation, motivation and work ethic – and of course a very good base of knowledge that has laid the foundations for your potential university study. You're in a great position!

Now, I'm sure that over the course of your final year at college/sixth form, you'll have been hounded with the ins and outs of the detailed process of applying for university and invitations to various open days to discuss which institution you're going to pick. In the midst of this, you'll have had your A-level exams to worry about, and as a result you've probably had little time to stop and think about whether the whole university experience is even the right thing for you.

Let me start by saying: University is not for everyone.
Some people decide that 18 years of education is more than enough for them, in which case going out and getting a job is perfectly respectable and exactly the right thing to do.

For some people's chosen careers, practical experience is much more preferable to employers than a university degree, in which case, you should absolutely go out into the big wide world and hone your craft! In other cases, there are other options such as apprenticeships available, which might be more suited to you. (I'll touch on these in a bit more detail shortly.)

If you decide that the world of work is the place for you rather than an extra three (or more) years sitting in lecture halls, this is a perfectly respectable decision and NO ONE can think less of you for it. In fact, neither myself nor my sister ever even considered university – now, I'm studying for my doctorate as well as lecturing undergraduates, and she is staying on for her master's degree – neither of us saw it coming, and now can't seem to leave!

If, however you're still undecided about whether this is the path you should be taking, perhaps the following advice might help you come to a decision (though at this point, I hope you've already settled on university as your chosen path, otherwise you'll be returning this book to the book shop!)

Are you only considering going because your friends are or you want to kill some time?

You'd be surprised that this is one of the most common reasons that people enrol on a university degree in the first instance. There's nothing wrong with wanting to stay with your friends from school and college, or indeed wanting to buy yourself some time before having to make any big career decisions. If this is what you're thinking, my only advice to you is to consider the other options? What job do you see yourself doing in the long run? Would you benefit from having a university degree, or is it a bit irrelevant to your career path? If so, you might like to consider the idea that earning money and sparing yourself student debt might be a better option for you than committing to three years study and a lot of money spent?

Which leads me on to my next point...

<u>Will a degree help you?</u>
Whilst some jobs directly specify the minimum requirement of a bachelor's degree, there are some occupations where a degree is totally irrelevant. If this is the case, you might want to weigh up the time and money that will be spent (as mentioned above) against the possible gains in getting a university degree. This is not at all to put you off – I've worked with several students who enrolled on a degree because they wanted the whole experience of living away, being independent and studying a subject they loved in more detail more than they wanted the actual qualification. If your situation allows, then this is of course an option for you – but unfortunately not everyone is that lucky, and some may have to take extra care in deciding whether enrolling on a university degree course is the right thing for them.

<u>Can you take on the student debt that comes with a degree?</u>
Without wishing to engage in a political rant (I'll spare you that!), university is no longer free, and comes at a very high cost. Unless you choose to self-fund your degree, or are being sponsored from another source, you will apply for a student loan, paid to you by the student loans company (SLC). There is a tuition fee loan to cover the cost of your studies (which can cost up to £9,250 a year) and a maintenance loan of varying amounts depending on your means and circumstances. I'm no money expert, and won't go into too much detail on this – but my advice to you is: don't see this loan as
actual money that you owe. Your student loan doesn't affect your credit rating, and you may never pay it all back. You will only start paying back your loan once you are earning above the repayment threshold – if you never work...you never pay!

At present, the amount that you pay is 9% (6% for postgraduate degrees) of the money you earn that is over the repayment threshold – so it's almost easier to think of this as a tax deduction on any future earnings as opposed to money that you actually owe.

The other side of things is the maintenance, and here is where it gets tricky for some people. Every student's personal situation, whether they are living along or with parents, is what we call "means tested" to determine which band of loan they are entitled to. Some are entitled to more or less money than others as a result of their circumstances. Usually a member of your family (parent or carer) is asked to submit information to the student loans company to verify which bracket you fall into. This is all managed via your student finance online account, and the process is quick and simple. (Just be sure to remind them to respond in time with the evidence needed! I know my mum needed a bit of prodding when I was applying for my student loan!)

It's important to keep in mind that generally, the amount of student maintenance loan that you are entitled to doesn't always fully cover the amount that you actually spend on rent, food, living costs etc. Living with others can reduce your rent, but this usually happens in your second or third years of study once you've settled into friendship groups. For your first year, if you choose to stay on campus, this will usually be in the "halls of residence", which are rented at a fixed price. Some students choose to get a job to make up for any potential shortfall in expenditure and income from the student loans company, but others choose not to. Whilst there are many support networks in place to prevent financial circumstances from standing in the way of anyone receiving higher education, it's worth keeping money in mind to save you any stress or anxiety later.

If you're a little unclear about the whole area of student finance, there is a whole chapter on it later.

<u>Could university be something that you can come back to later?</u>
The typical "gap year" comes to mind when suggesting that university is something that can be revisited. The fact is, between your mandatory education and the start of your elective study can be a fantastic time to see the world and experience new things. It can help you to learn new life skills that will mean you will have an easier time of settling into the swing of university independence when it comes to it. When you're employed in a full-time job, you will rarely get the opportunity to have this amount of time off to check things off your bucket list, so if a gap year is tempting you – give it some serious consideration.

There is the other option of going out to work for a few years before commencing university study. This will help with your finances, but you may also find that, if gaining a degree gives you more skills and knowledge to apply to your place of work, your employer may consider funding all or part of your tuition cost. Perhaps you could study for your degree on a part-time basis, whilst continuing with your professional work alongside?

<u>Are there other options that suit you and your chosen career more than a university degree?</u>
If a three-year university degree isn't quite right for you, but you still want to continue learning, there are plenty of other options:

Degree apprenticeship
Think of a degree apprenticeship as a combination of university study and work. The big plus of this is gaining a degree without the debt! Typically, you will work three or four days a week and study at university for the other two or three. Why is there no debt, I hear you ask? Well, as well as receiving a salary for your paid work, your employer and the government will cover the cost of your tuition fees. "This is too good to be true!" (I hear you say) Well, of course

the negative is that you may find yourself much less engaged in the university experience and wider study community, and the other down side is that this is a fairly new scheme. Having only been launched in 2015, degree apprenticeships are not all that common, and are more commonly found in the science, technology and engineering industries. However, do keep a look out if this sounds like the option for you, and remember that unlike university where you apply through UCAS, in the case of degree apprenticeships, you apply direct to your potential employer. My only piece of advice in this case is, be mindful of what the conditions are when applying for a degree apprenticeship within a particular company.

In some cases, you may be required to work for that company for a period of time after you've completed your official studies — so always read terms and conditions carefully, and know the full details of what you're applying for.

Higher apprenticeship
This is essentially a degree apprenticeship with the difference being that you are awarded a level 4 or 5 qualification at the end, as opposed to a full university bachelor's degree. With this in mind, the focus of a higher apprenticeship focuses more your professional training and preparation to enter your chosen industry workplace than the academic side of your work. There is no guarantee of a job placement at the end of a higher apprenticeship, but it massively boosts your employability, and many students find that they are offered a permanent role within the same company or they find a role much more easily within another organisation.

Foundation degree
A foundation degree is typically organised by universities and employers working in partnerships and once again aims to train you "on the job" for a role in your chosen industry.

You will combine study with work and will achieve a foundation degree at the end (which is basically two thirds of a full honours degree) Once you graduate, you can move into full time employment, but some students choose to stay on for an extra year in order to convert their foundation degree into a full degree. Aside from the qualification, the other difference between this is and a degree apprenticeship is the fact that you apply through UCAS rather than to your potential employer, and you are entitled to student finance to cover your tuition fees/maintenance. Foundation degrees are much more common than degree apprenticeships, so this could be a very good alternative for you if a degree apprenticeship is not yet available in your chosen field.

Traineeship

A traineeship is typically a much shorter course designed to train a student up for a particular job. This is typically the option for those who might not have the qualifications for an apprenticeship, but it is still a very respectable and viable option. You don't get paid for traineeships, but your expenses will usually be covered.

Traineeships give you vital experience in the workplace that looks fabulous on your CV when applying for future jobs!

Internship/other form of work experience

Internships are great if you want to try out a job before committing to a permanent role in that field. They are usually more for graduates, but there are some schemes available as an alternative to a degree. Some internships can be quite competitive, but they look great on your CV and are usually paid.

Work experience is less formal and can be organised directly between yourself and an employer. There is no guarantee of a job at the end of it, but again, it really improves your employment prospects and shows a real determination to expand your learning and professionalism in preparation for a permanent role.

Entry level jobs
You probably won't need me to explain this to you – but entry level jobs are jobs that are specifically targeted at those who have just left school/college. There may be the requirement of good grades in certain subjects, but there may also be no requirements other than professionalism, energy and enthusiasm. Some of these roles might be full time and permanent, some may be part time – some may also have the option for career progression within the company...so you may just find yourself set for life if this is the road you want to take! If you're looking for an entry level job, you can find these yourself on job sites, or register with an agency who will search for you.

Go it alone!
If you have experience, ideas and an entrepreneurial spirit, then why not consider starting your own business? This is of course a mammoth task that shouldn't be taken lightly, but you don't have to look very far to find success stories of people who have started to build their own business as an alternative to university. Many banks offer good financial advice in starting a business, and can provide designated business accounts without account fees for start-up enterprises. It's worth taking the time to put together a full and comprehensive business plan, outlining your intentions and projections before approaching any other parties for advice or assistance.

It's important to remember that not all businessmen and women wear suits – living off of croissants and black coffee in Canary Wharf is not the sole requirement of building a business empire...with a good idea, work ethic and determination, anything is possible!

THE APPLICATION MIND-SET

If you've got your heart set on the university path, it's important to keep a few things in mind before embarking upon your application:

When I attended my lecturer training course, I was told this (and I'm paraphrasing of course):
"Now that many universities across the country have expanded to allow them to take on more students, it's becoming more important than ever that we not only make a good pitch to students to make them choose us in the first place, but remain as the student's university of choice if their A-level results are better than they had expected"
So, what does this mean for you?

Whilst you may want to attend that particular university, they also want you! (Lots of prospective students lose sight of this) Your university has to deliver an engaging and inspiring pitch to you, just as much as you have to impress them enough to offer you a place. Don't feel powerless in applying for any university – everybody's applications have value and they are lucky to receive yours!

Remember that "clearing" can change everything – You might not have heard of the "clearing" process. If not, I'll explain it quickly for you now:
"Clearing" is essentially a period of time before the academic year has started, where prospective university students are matched to university places that haven't yet been filled. You might have heard of the slightly more negative side of clearing, where students' exams haven't quite gone to plan. In this case, they haven't quite got the grades for their university of choice, so apply to others with lower grade thresholds through the clearing process. BUT – this process can also be flipped. Sometimes, exams go much

better than extended, and students find themselves able to attend a more competitive university that they might not have thought to apply to in the first place. This is why clearing can be both an exciting and a dangerous time for universities. Whilst they may well see a sudden rush of new students who hadn't initially applied, they may also find that many decline their offers of a place in order to attend a different institution. Never lose your self-esteem and remember that universities are fighting to keep you, just as much as you may feel you are fighting for a place!

You are an asset to whatever university you apply for and decide to attend.
I can't really put this any other way, but without students – there would be no universities. By deciding on this higher education path, you are playing a part in the continued future of higher education. By getting your degree, you will have a positive impact on whatever industry or field of study you have chosen.

You have put yourself in the position to make a real difference – and we all applaud you for it!

HOW AM I SUPPOSED TO WRITE ABOUT MYSELF? PERSONAL STATEMENT TIPS AND POINTERS

There are two main elements to any university application; exam results (or relevant experience), and a personal statement. This is either sent through UCAS to your university of choice, or direct to the university you're applying to as per their own admissions process. A personal statement is what it says on the tin; the chance for you to speak for yourself, rather than your exam results talking for you. It's your personal statement that usually results in you being offered an interview/audition or not, and from this interview, you could potentially be given an unconditional or conditional offer (that is based on either the achievement of certain grades in your A-levels, or the fulfilment of other criteria.)

A personal statement is both one of the easiest and hardest essays you'll ever write. Why — well, nobody's the subject of "you" better than yourself...academically you're already the world's leading expert — but writing about your personal strengths and skills is something that some people find very challenging. The most common trait I've seen in students writing personal statements is that they always overthink it. It doesn't need to be a difficult task, in fact, if you simply write what comes naturally to you, then you're bound to have a very easy time of it! It is hard to blow your own trumpet, but that's exactly what you have to do here!
In case you're having a bit of difficulty putting pen to paper, I'll take you through a few tips and pointers:

Don't overcomplicate the opening – I've seen many personal statements which start with quotes from famous people, a full explanation of the whys and wherefores of their particular field of study and plenty more. Keep the introduction short and to the point. State who you are with a short background, and above all why you feel passionate to continue your studies in a particular subject.

Let your enthusiasm do the talking – Don't tell the person reading your personal statement what they already know. What I mean by this is, they don't need to know what a leading professional thought about a particular area of study, they want to know why YOU want to further this work and why it is important to you that you are part of the continued development within the industry.

Always direct your personal statement to a particular university and course on offer – Mentioning why studying that particular course at that particular institution is bound to capture the reader's attention. It helps them to see that you have weighed up all the options available and are certain that the university you are applying to is the right one for you. It shows that you've thought about how the university can help you develop, but also how you'd fit into the university community and be a part of student life.

Talk about something that is inspiring you within your chosen field of study and the industry that this leads to. Do you already have a certain career in mind? If so, state why you are passionate and motivated to enter this particular field. Do you have new ideas or want to change an existing process for the better? No matter how big your ambition, make sure you say it.

Avoid cliché phrases — You'd be surprised by how often we see the phrases "ever since I was a child", "for as long as I can remember" and "I've loved (whatever the subject is) all my life" Reading these now, you might be thinking that these phrases sound a little bit cringe worthy — and to tell you the truth, they are a bit! As well as being a bit tired and overused, be aware that some of these phrases also make it sound like you've already retired and are looking back on your career as a fond but distant memory. By saying "all my life, I've loved to *read various works of classic literature* (for example), you're making it sound as if you've read all that you need to know and want to know. It has a very "final" tone to it, that comes across as closeminded. The fact is, you're at the very start of your journey, and it's far better to write about the excitement that being in that position holds for you. Instead, you can write something like "Classic literature is a great passion of mine, and I am very excited by the prospect of studying this field more closely, so I can make a positive and meaningful impact on the industry as a whole over the course of my career" This oozes excitement, enthusiasm and a desire to succeed in a fresh and vibrant way.

Follow a circle structure with your overall writing — Some people would call this "the necklace approach", others will call it a "narrative arch (or circle)" but it can be a very nice touch to end where you started. It helps to give your writing a sense of coherency and structure without actually following the flow of a full on academic piece of writing. If you started with why you love your chosen subject, then perhaps you can end with something like "and it is for these reasons that I feel so passionate about *architecture* (for instance), and I hope that you are able to help me further my knowledge and skill at university, so I can bring this passion to the industry for many years to come"

Ask yourself: 'Does what I'm writing add value?' - This was a great little pearl of wisdom that my mum actually gave me when I was writing my own personal statement. When you're writing about yourself, you can easily get caught up in including the occasional piece of irrelevant detail — and as impressive as your level 3 swimming award is, it's probably not really applicable to your desire to apply for a business management degree, for instance. Repeat this phrase in your head as you're putting pen to paper: "does what I'm writing add value?" If it does, then write away — if not, then save for a more conversational forum, like your university interview!

No matter how impressive your CV or experience is, your personal statement holds the key to securing you an interview/audition at your chosen institution. A lot of tutorials advise you to "try to be unique", but I believe that every person is unique, and as such, every personal statement will be. What I advise instead is to be honest and enthusiastic. When thinking about the "honest" element: if you've overcome something substantial to get to this point, then do make mention of it! Don't fake your interest in a subject, otherwise you'll be stuck doing a degree for three years in a topic that doesn't inspire you all that much. If you truly love what you do, then let that love shine through! The same thing goes with enthusiasm. If there is a particular part of your topic that interests you, then focus on that – it may just help to set you apart from the other applications and help you to come across as someone with a very real interest in a specialist area who already knows exactly where they want to fit into a particular industry.

Your school or college will usually provide you with lots of help and support in putting your personal statement together, however, please always keep in mind that nobody knows the topic of "you" better than YOU. Whilst we can all provide you with help and advice in what to write and how to write it, this is your opportunity to showcase and put into writing your biggest achievements to date, and let your passion and enthusiasm for your chosen subject shine through above all else! Writing a personal statement should feel like an enjoyable exercise – not a chore. By the time you've uploaded the finished article to UCAS, you will have laid your own foundations for your successful acceptance into the university of your choice, and you'll be well on your way to achieving your dream career. You're now just a few exams away from that guaranteed university place and the start of a very new and exciting chapter in your life. Savour the moment, and get ready for one hell of a ride!

STUDENT FINANCE EXPLAINED (BECAUSE MONEY MAKES THE WORLD GO ROUND!)

By the time you're thinking about applying for student finance, you will have already settled on the university you're going to attend, and if this is the case, CONGRATULATIONS.

The next step before your enrolment day is to ensure that all of your finances are in order.

As I touched on briefly at the very beginning of the book, all eligible students will be entitled to support from the student loans company. Whether you are eligible for a student loan depends on a variety of factors. At present, you are eligible for a student loan if:

- You are studying a recognised course with a recognised university
- You're studying full-time (but this doesn't necessarily have to be a bachelor's degree. There are many other recognised courses, as I touched on before) NB. You can be eligible if you're studying part time, but you must be studying for a recognised qualification, and your "course intensity" must be 25% or more. Course intensity means how much of your course you complete each year when compared with the full-time mode of study. In other words, you must be completing at least 25% of the full course each year.
- You are studying for your first higher education qualification (if you've studied before, even on a self-funded basis, you may not be eligible)

If you already have a degree, there are a few limited cases where you may still be eligible for funding. This generally depends on what subject your degree is in.

There is no upper age limit for the receipt of student finance. There are several residency criteria that enable both UK and non-UK nationals to apply for student finance.

If you have any doubt about your eligibility, then it's always best to visit the gov.uk website for further advice and guidance.

WHAT YOU'LL GET
There are two main types of loan that the student loans company offer; a tuition fee loan, and a maintenance loan:

TUITION FEE LOAN:
This is made up of the cost of your tuition fees (which will be in the region of £9,000 per year) and will be paid direct to your university of choice by the student loans company. You will never see this money, and for an undergraduate degree, you will not be responsible for the payment of your tuition fee loan to your place of study.

MAINTENANCE LOAN:
Every student who is eligible for a tuition fee loan is eligible for at least some size of maintenance loan. However, unlike the tuition fee loan, the size of the loan you are entitled to is not fixed. How much money you are paid as a maintenance loan depends on your place of study and your household income. According to the student loans company, the average amount received by students as a maintenance loan

is £6,480 per year, but you can receive up to £11,672 (in 2020), depending on your circumstances. These circumstances are; your household income, where you will be studying and where you will be living (you will be entitled a higher maintenance loan if you are living away from home for the duration of your studies for instance.)

When applying for your maintenance loan, evidence of your household income will need to be supplied, alongside your course information and your living arrangements. Usually your parent/guardian would be the person to provide this information, and once you have entered their contact details on your application, the student loans company will get in touch with them directly (usually by email), to request the relevant documents. It's not always the case that university applicants are living with parents. Some may be living alone, and have dependents of their own – and the process takes this into account. If this is the case, you will supply your own financial income.

As I mentioned before, be sure to remind whoever is completing this for you (if it's not you personally!) to do so as soon as possible, as a slow response can cause a delay in the overall process.

Unlike tuition fee loans, maintenance loans will be paid direct to you, usually in three instalments throughout the academic year – so be sure to manage your money wisely!

One thing to consider is that, when taking into account your household income to determine your appropriate loan amount, the student loans company is assuming that your parents or guardians are able (and willing) to contribute to the cost of your studies. In some instances, this isn't the case, and it is important to keep the student loans company informed of any changes in circumstance that means you are unable to support yourself financially with the amount that you have been allocated.

REPAYMENTS:

With "loan" being the key word, this money will need to be paid back. However, there are many caveats to repayments of student loans, and you'll be pleased to know that the process is actually quite friendly and generous!

As I touched on briefly before, the key thing to remember with the repayment of student loans is that you only start to make repayments when you earn above the repayment threshold. These thresholds can change, and it's always worth visiting the gov.uk website to check what these are.

For an undergraduate loan, you pay 9% of the amount you earn OVER THE THRESHOLD.
At present (in 2020), the repayment thresholds and examples of these are as follows:

GOV.UK EXAMPLES (AS OF 2020):

PLAN 1
(For eligible students who started an undergraduate course in the UK before 1st September 2012)

REPAYMENT THRESHOLD: £372 a week, or £1,615 a month – before tax and any other deductions

CASE 1:
You're paid monthly and your income changes each month. This month your income was £2,000, which is over the Plan 1 monthly threshold of £1,615.

Your income was £385 over the threshold (£2,000 minus £1,615). You will pay back £34 (9% of £385) this month

CASE 2:
Your annual income is £27,000 and you're paid a regular monthly wage. This means that each month your income is £2,250 (£27,000 divided by 12). This is over the Plan 1 monthly threshold of £1,615.

Your income is £635 over the threshold (£2,250 minus £1,615). You will pay back £57 (9% of £635) each month.

INTEREST ON PLAN 1
You currently pay interest of 1.1% on Plan 1.

PLAN 2
(For eligible students who started an undergraduate course in the UK on or after 1st September 2012)

REPAYMENT THRESHOLD: £511 a week, or £2,214 a month - before tax and any other deductions

CASE 1:
You're paid weekly and your income changes each week. This week your income was £600, which is over the Plan 2 weekly threshold of £511.

Your income was £89 over the threshold (£600 minus £511). You will pay back £8 (9% of £89) this week.

CASE 2:
Your annual income is £28,800 and you are paid a regular monthly wage. This means that each month your income is £2,400 (£28,800 divided by 12). This is over the Plan 2 monthly threshold of £2,214.

Your income is £186 over the threshold (£2,400 minus £2,214). You will pay back £16 (9% of £186) each month.

INTEREST ON PLAN 2
While you're studying, interest is 5.4%.

This is made up of the Retail Price Index (RPI) plus 3%. RPI is currently set at 2.4%.

This rate applies until the 5 April after you finish or leave your course, or for the first 4 years of your course if you're studying part-time, unless the RPI changes. After that, your interest rate depends on your income in the current tax year.

If you're self-employed, your income is the total income amount on your Self-Assessment form.

If you're an employee, your income is your taxable pay plus any pension contributions, minus any benefits you get from your employer that are taxed through payroll (ask your employer if you're not sure) If you have more than one job in a year, your interest rate will be based on your combined income from all your jobs.

INTEREST RATES:

Your annual income	Interest rate
£26,575 or less	RPI (currently 2.4%)
£26,576 to £47,835	RPI (currently 2.4%), plus up to 3%
Over £47,835	RPI (currently 2.4%), plus 3%

Examples reference: Gov.uk. (Updated 2020). Repaying your student loan. Available: https://www.gov.uk/repaying-your-student-loan/what-you-pay. Last accessed 8th April 2020.

If you never earn over the repayment threshold, you never pay.

There may also be cases where you overpay your student loan. This may have happened if you earn over the repayment threshold in one particular month, but your annual income is under the threshold. If this is the case, you are entitled to a refund, and can claim at the end of the appropriate tax year
by calling the repayment line: 0300 100 0611 *NB. Refunds must be requested over the phone.*

There are other ways to get in touch with the Student Loans Company, including via social media channels (would you believe it!) for repayment queries. Direct social media messaging on Facebook and Twitter is open on weekdays, and in my experience, the messages are picked up very quickly.

NOW FOR A BIT OF MYTH-BUSTING!

A lot of students worry that as soon as they reach that repayment threshold, they'll start receiving bills from student finance in the post — but don't worry. If you are employed, your employer will deduct the appropriate amount from your salary each month — so you never "see" this money. With this in mind, it's far easier to think of the student loan as a type of tax that is taken off your earnings alongside other deductions. If you're self-employed and fill out a self-assessment tax return, HMRC will work this out for you, and the amount payable will be encompassed into your tax bill. In any case, the student loan's company will be notified when you start to earn above the repayment threshold, and you will receive a letter in the post informing you that your repayments have kicked in. If you are working for somebody else, there's no need to worry about specifically informing anyone of your earnings, and if you're self-employed, your self-assessment tax return is the way you complete your notification.

While student loan repayments are undoubtedly the part of the university experience that is the least enjoyable to think about, the process is very user friendly. Don't panic! You can also check the total amount that you owe by logging in to your student finance account online – but this comes with a warning. Sometimes the amount you see might seem quite alarming, but remember to think of this as a "graduate tax" as opposed to actual debt!

And...an added bonus is that after 30 years, all the money owed is wiped – whether you've paid the whole lot back or not! Unless you're earning a high salary and any late repayments will increase interest payments, I wouldn't readily advice that you pay large chunks off of the amount of money you owe. Sticking with the repayment plan is a far and reliable way of making necessary repayments that are proportionate to your income.

My final piece of myth-busting wisdom is: Student loans do not appear on your individual credit report. Given that they don't appear on your credit report, they do not directly affect your credit score. "What's a credit report and score?" I hear you ask. Well, the best way I have heard a credit report described is as a kind of financial CV. If you've maintained a good history of paying credit card bills and other debits on time, this would culminate in a good credit report. If you've maxed out credit cards or been consistently late with payments, then suddenly your credit report doesn't look quite so attractive. The credit score is a three-digit number generated from the credit report. The better the report, the higher the number and the more attractive you are to lenders. Obviously, it goes without saying that a lower credit score means that a lender would be taking a greater risk in lending money to you, and as such, you might be ineligible for certain types of borrowing (mortgages, credit cards etc.) Financial history can stay on your credit report for up to six years, so the good news is; you can improve your credit score in the long run!

Now, given that a student loan doesn't appear on your credit report, it cannot affect your credit score. However, lenders may ask about any student loan you have as part of an affordability check...so don't be alarmed!

In short, never let finance put you off achieving a higher education. There are always ways to make it happen, and plenty of support available from your university and third-party organisations should you need assistance later on.

ADDITIONAL TIPS AND POINTERS
Your student status makes you eligible for a variety of different perks and benefits. Be sure to make use of the following:

Council tax exemption – If you're living away from home and renting a property outside of the university campus that is only occupied by full-time students, then your property is classified as 'exempt' from council tax payments. All occupants will need to get a student status letter from your university (which is usually available from your student services department) that you should send to your local council to clarify your exemption. If you are living in student halls, the property is exempt automatically. (At least that's one less thing to worry about!)
If your whole property isn't automatically exempt (i.e. if some people living with you are not full-time students), you yourself can be 'disregarded.' This means that the council tax is calculated as if you don't live there, and can result in

the person who has to pay the tax being entitled to some discounts. If this is the case, be sure to still send a student status letter to the council so they can calculate the new amount payable for your property.

Student discount card — This is an absolute MUST! A student discount card can be purchased online or sometimes direct from your student union. This card used to be called an NUS card, but is now called a TOTUM card, and also acts as official proof of ID. Membership starts at £14.99 per year (in 2020) but this money is WELL worth spending. Other tariffs and membership categories are available, so it's worth checking out the other options. Shops and restaurants have great student reductions (including Topshop, Pizza Express, New Look and even Apple and Co-op supermarkets!), but remember that these discounts aren't always clearly advertised. With this in mind, it's worth making "do you give student discount?" your staple phrase at any till point. You might just find yourself making a surprise saving! I made back my £14.99 almost straight away with a 25% student reduction on my Gourmet Burger Bill! Don't forget online services also offer student rates, including Amazon Prime and Apple Music — so always check what discounts are available before you buy!

Oyster and Railcards — If you're using public transport regularly, purchasing an applicable railcard is a great opportunity to further save money. If you live in a London borough during term time and are in full-time education at a TFL-registered institution, you will be entitled to an 18+ student oyster card. (There are other eligible courses, so it's worth checking what you're entitled to.) This Oyster card gives you a 30% discount on adult-rate travelcards and bus and tram pass season tickets. This is a massive saving — particularly if you purchase a monthly or yearly season ticket. This is available for purchase from the TFL website for £20.

The other option is the 16-25 railcard which is open to anyone aged 16-25 (or above) as long as you are in full-time education. This can be purchased most quickly online, but can also be purchased at any staffed ticket office (as long as you bring along a completed application form and your correct ID documents — see website for details) It costs £30 and gives you a 1/3 saving on rail fairs throughout Great Britain for a year. A 3-year railcard is also available at £70, but can only be purchased online. Your 16-25 railcard allows you to save on Standard Anytime and Off-Peak fares, as well as advance tickets, and there are also many partners to the railcard scheme which offer you further discounts on restaurants, experiences and other services.

I have both a student Oyster card and a railcard —and I use them on every journey.

THERE IS ALSO ANOTHER PLUS TO HAVING BOTH:

You can link your railcard to your Oyster account and can save 34% on pay as you go off-peak fares (on London Underground, Overground, TFL rail and most

National Rail Services) by adding your railcard to your

18+ Oyster card. To link the two cards, you need to take both cards to a staffed ticket office and a member of staff will link the two cards. The discount will be valid until the rail card expires.

Other methods of travel including coach lines (National Express/Megabus and more) and even various river bus lines offer student discount, with the stipulation of having a valid NUS/TOTUM card. However, sometimes journeys must be booked a certain number of days in advance for the discount to be redeemable.

Apply for any appropriate scholarships and bursaries – Always keep an eye out for any funding that may be available, both within your university and outside. Some universities have internal scholarships available (and I'll talk about this in a bit more detail later), but there are also external trusts that give money to students studying in specific fields. Some trusts are specifically for university tuition fees, whilst others are more general and support the cost of studies/materials/other research costs, as well as the cost of the tuition itself. I actually received some funding from an external trust fund that supports music students for my degree. There are also some trusts that support students from (or with a connection to) a particular location – so make sure you do your research and see if there are any sources of funding that you are eligible to apply for...nothing ventured, nothing gained!

If your university has a money card scheme, make sure you use it! – Some universities (usually in conjunction with any resident book shop) offer a scheme where a certain amount of money is loaded onto a card each year which can be spent on study materials at that particular book shop. In the universities that I have studied at and worked within, this has been called an 'Aspire' card, but this may differ between institutions. The study materials on offer in resident book shops ranges from reading list books to laptops and sportswear – so make sure you spend any money that you are allocated wisely!

ENROLMENT & THAT FIRST DAY

I'll never forget my first day of university! Granted, my situation was a little away from the norm, but perhaps if I tell you my experiences, you might feel a little less alone.

I was sixteen years old when I first walked the corridors of The University of West London's London College of Music. I remember that first time I had to attend the campus to enrol — it was one of the strangest things I think I've ever done. The whole of the university was bristling with signs and leaflets and students in the brightest yellow t-shirts I think I've ever seen — some enthusiastic, and some not quite so much! I remember looking at the large pull-up banners plastered with pictures of happy students lying on the grass reading with their friends, or posing in the middle of walking purposefully with a rucksack and thinking that it seemed like some kind of wartime propaganda — you know, like those "We can do it/your country needs you" posters, but with less headscarves and moustaches and far more fresher's logos and preppy clothing. I had to present ID documents, exam certificates, pick up handbooks, go on tours and of course, pose awkwardly for the obligatory student card photo, which would turn out to be the point of much ridicule over the following three years.

On the subject of ID cards — always take a mental snapshot of that moment that you smile for that photo — because who knows what you'll look like in three years! I've seen different hair colours, piercings, tattoos, and people who have smiled gawkily as a fresh-faced 18-year-old looking 45 by the time they leave the campus for the last time! This happened to a friend of mine, and I kid you not, he was clean shaven with quite an impressive amount of hair when he enrolled, and by the end, he was bearded...but balding! (How do you manage that?!)

Anyway, I promise you'll laugh — and even if you don't physically change at all, the knowledge in that brain of yours will be far greater.

So, savour that second!

I'm sure I'm not the only person to have felt this way at enrolment, but it felt like something that I was just enduring for that moment in time. In all honesty, I felt like the whole university thing was never actually going to start. In my head, I was saying "sure, you're enrolling now, but it's not as if you're actually ever going to have to come here again — let alone take a class or sit an exam" and here I am now, in this strange loop of always returning to education in some shape or form! What you learn never truly leaves you, and when you leave university, it won't just be with a degree — but it will be with a thirst for knowledge that keeps teasing you into wanting to know more and more about your chosen field of study.

Something else about enrolment was very strange, and that was the way in which everyone seems to size each other up in a totally non-threating but very intense manner. The truth is, until you sit in that first class, you never know who you're going to end up working with. I don't think I saw anybody I met at enrolment again. One thing you have to remember is; people have come from far and wide to attend the institution that you now find yourself holding an ID card for. This isn't like school where, if you're in the local catchment area, you get a place. No, this is far different – and in a way, far more exciting. For the overwhelming majority of people, this is not just a new place of study, but a new part of the world, with new shops, new pubs, new restaurants, and even a new home. All students have actively chosen to study at your university, so with that in mind, you already have something in common with everybody you pass as you walk through campus! Go out and find that new local pub without the staff who've know you since the age of five and comment on how grown up you are every time you order alcohol instead of a J20! This is your chance to make your mark on the design of the landscape around you, with as much or as little input from anyone else as you would like.

On this topic, I have to share a little insight with you, which might provide you with some reassurance. Recently, as a result of staff sickness, I had to take on the lecturing of some new first year classes. I didn't know any of them, and this must have only been six weeks into the academic year – and honestly, I was more scared than they were! I was just so amazed that in six short weeks this class seemed like they had been together for six years. The dynamic was so equal and everybody seemed to have their place – and be happy in it! Even people who seemed a little less confident were not alone. Whilst it would be naïve, and frankly silly to assume that this is always the case (of course there are going to be some teething problems) I just want to show you that it is possible to settle, and settle very quickly! Take it from someone who was never the most natural in social situations – **you will be ok.**

Just one final thing to say on enrolment before I move onto the ups and downs of that first day:

You can never go wrong!

Not least because of the often-ridiculous amount of signage that makes a corridor look like a motorway, but also because everybody understands that going wrong is a part of this new journey for you. I've walked the campus as that shy and panicked student, and now, just because I wear a staff lanyard instead of a student ID card, that feeling hasn't gone away forever. I will always remember feeling small and insignificant and lost – and so, I share a smile with students who look like they're feeling the same way...and that's the beauty of university – your staff are your colleagues, and we remember what it felt like. In fact, lots of staff are studying for advanced degrees whilst teaching undergraduates. In many ways, it's a carousel. Staff and students alike – we all just go around and round...it's just that we've been on it a little longer!

I remember happily milling about on enrolment day, totally oblivious that I was supposed to be in a course meeting at that very moment. So, I LEGGED it up three flights of stairs, sweaty, stressed and scared...only to find about fifteen other people doing the same.

We are all here for you, and making mistakes is just part of the fun.

In interests of being honest with you, I'd like to share with you some of my biggest mistakes and regrets as they arise (and this will be a theme across the whole book) My first big regret actually concerns enrolment, and it is this:

I wish I hadn't run off as soon as I did what I had to do.

It's so tempting, and I know...because I did it! If you're quite an extroverted people person, then you might have a slightly easier time of the whole "first time on campus" experience — but if you aren't, you might struggle, as I did. I distinctly remember grabbing everything I had to take, going through all the different checkpoints and presenting/collecting documents, and as soon as I'd finished, running out of the building faster than you could say "student finance." Whilst this was great at the time, and it got me out of what I found in all honesty to be quite a tense and nervy situation, it made going back for the first lecture all the more difficult. You might not be one of those people who wants to go to every fresher's activity on the list (and believe me, they'll be plenty!) You might not want to go to any at all! BUT, the best thing I can possibly advise you to do before you sprint back home and jump right back in to that Netflix series is to walk the corridors at least once. You might know your timetable already, in which case this would be a fantastic opportunity to find your classrooms (at least for the first day) so you don't have to panic later on. If not, just walk the halls and get to grips with the set-up. If there are particular "blocks" then know where they start and end. Is there a room labelling system?

In the London College of Music, a room might be labelled like this:
BY.02.007

In this case, BY is stands for Byron, which is the name of one of the teaching blocks/zones

02 is floor 2

007 is room 7

This is very much the same for most other universities I have come across — and if not, something fairly similar will be in place.

Use the time after enrolment to get to grips with this. If you meet someone friendly, they might want to join you, but if not, just take half an hour to do it yourself. You'll be so glad you did later, and you might even be able to help someone else.

Contrary to my insistence that the whole university experience was never going to start — it actually did — for me, on the 23rd September 2013...and no, I didn't need to look that up! (It's forever etched in my memory!) After a longer summer holiday than I was used to, I remember getting all flustered about what I actually needed to bring, so in the end I ended up packing enough equipment to last for the whole term, let alone 2 hours!

So, first lecture: unless otherwise stated, bring a notebook and a pencil case (and any learning materials that you may have been given/told to get in advance)

My first lecture was called 'General Musicianship' and whilst I had always imagined university lectures to be in those massive theatres with those chairs that have little fold-up tables, I was amazed that this was just like every other school lesson (except for the fact that I wasn't wearing a uniform!) Teachers are your colleagues and as such, you use their first names — and it's ok to ask them about their weekends — in fact, they'll like it! This lecture was very much a "whiteboard and pen" setup that I'm sure you're all so used to from school, and in a way, I found that quite comforting. One thing to be mindful of is the fact that the lectures may feel quite basic to start with. This is just so that the playing field is level for all students before any formal assignments are set. So, before you feel like the degree you've just enrolled onto is more boring than watching grass grow, or far too difficult to finish – it won't be like this forever. Just think, whilst you might have roughly the same A levels as the person sitting next to you in the class, there could be many different options and courses of study within that one qualification. I suppose it's like two people both studying history; but one has studied the English Civil War and the other has studied the Tudors – both have the qualification, but that doesn't mean that they know anything about what the other person has studied.

To this end, the first couple of weeks might feel a bit slow or fast depending on the situation – but the main thing to remember is...**don't form any immediate judgements or make any spur of the moment decisions!** Of course, first impressions count, and I have no doubt that you are all very good at judging situations – however, bear in mind that this experience is unlike any situation you have faced so far, so you might need to give it a little more time.

In this first lecture, you will usually be given a "module study guide" or something similar, which outlines the objectives, assignments and learning material for the module. It will detail who your lecturer is, and their contact details, as well as any other support staff and guidelines of what to do if something isn't quite going your way.

Now, as far as possible (and believe me, I've fallen victim to this a number of times) don't turn straight to the assignment page and panic! I know how tempting it is...but try to resist panic reading, and let your lecturer explain each part to you. Each module has to be "approved" by an education authority/quality assurance team, and because of this, the assignment description can often be written in a very "matter of fact" manner that doesn't explain the full scope of how that particular assessment can be completed. Reading this can leave you feeling clueless – but it's something you can refer to if you need to be reminded of the core objectives of the module later on.

So, now that you have all of your learning materials – the next step is immersing yourself in that first lecture. Fair warning, not all of it will make sense – and that's ok! I remember these "general musicianship" classes as if they were yesterday...before every class I'd call into the Sainsbury's petrol station on the walk in and buy a packet of jelly babies, which I would then try to eat silently at the back of the class. The sweets themselves weren't the issue – but those bags are the crinkliest things I've ever come across! Anyway, I remember being in awe of the ability to bring in a coffee to class and no one would bat an eyelid, or being able to take notes on a laptop without the threat of having it confiscated by a draconian head teacher – and that's part of the reason that I wanted to write this book...because no one teaches you this culture, this new way of life – and if you have to spend your first semester worrying about getting to grips with these boundaries and new ways of working, then that's a term of unnecessary worry when you should be hitting the ground running.

I realise that, over the course of that first lecture, your mind is probably on anything but the content of the lesson itself (and as lecturers, we're all aware of that too!) The best thing you can do to help yourself is take short notes and write down anything that you don't understand straight away, so you can address the problem before it reappears later. Your university will most likely have an online portal (generally it's called Blackboard – I'll explain a bit more in the next chapter.) where lecturers can upload any slides/learning materials from that particular lecture. Make sure to keep an eye on this. I often found that getting home, making a cup of coffee and going through the lecture again at my own pace whilst referring to my learning materials often answered any questions that I had stuck in my mind.

The main takeaway is; don't make any fast judgements of that first lecture. Turn up, make notes (but not too many!), smile and relax. Start off on the right footing and set the tone for a very successful outcome.

Oh...and one last thing for this chapter. You don't have to put your hand up and ask to go to the toilet – I learned this the hard way!

SO I'M TWO WEEKS IN...NOW WHAT?

Congratulations! This is a massive milestone in your university journey. To put this into a little bit of perspective from my experience as both a student and a staff member, the first two weeks are one of the most challenging parts of any degree - and you've already overcome it! Now, if you can get to grips with a possible house move, a new building, a new area, new people, more challenging work, and being independent both physically and financially, you can get through anything – right?!

Please remember this. When you have doubts in your own ability later – and if I'm honest, you will most likely reach a low point at some time or other – you must remember the magnitude of what you achieved in such a short time. Think of it like this, most adults never relocate, move in with strangers, start a new course of study and perhaps get a job at the same time – OF COURSE THEY DON'T! They might do it one bit at a time over a period of months or maybe even longer. This is a MASSIVE achievement, and everyone handles it differently. Staff are always aware of that, and there are always support networks in place for this very reason, should you ever need them.

Now, two weeks into my university journey I remember I still maintained the mind-set that I was never going to see the end of it...and this is completely normal (and expected!) However, most semesters are only 14 or 15 weeks long – so about a 7th of your first semester has already gone! (How's that for a scary thought?!) One thing you will notice is that, as a first-year student, time will seem to pass very, VERY slowly...but once you get to third year, you'll be wishing for those weeks to SLOW DOWN! What's really strange is that during your first year, you're probably going out, seeing friends, navigating a new city, as well as undertaking your studies – and yet you're wishing for time to speed up! It seems totally opposite – but that's university.

So, here's my advice for the two-week mark (from where I went wrong as a student and from what I now see as a staff member):

If you haven't already done so, make sure you register with a local GP practice and dentist if you're living away from home (and work out where they are in your local area.) You may never need an appointment, but going through the administration procedure of joining as a patient can be very tricky if you're unwell or in pain, and can delay you being allocated an appointment – so make sure you do this early. There are also very good options for remote healthcare that offer digital appointments via video conference. Some GP practices use an app called LIVI that offers this service to its patients free of charge, whilst other apps offer pay as you go digital appointments. (I recently discovered LIVI myself, and a doctor started a video call with me just 8 minutes later!) I recommend downloading a GP app and setting it up, just in case you may need it.

Make your emergency details known – By now you will hopefully have made some friends on your course/met your flatmates. It's always worth passing on your emergency contact details (parents/next of kin) to someone you're in regular contact with, just in case they're needed! It's also important to remember that many mobile phones now have the option to create a "medical ID." You can list any medications you're taking/any health conditions, and flag any contacts that can be used in an emergency. Failing that, the old trick of typing "ICE" (**I**n **C**ase of **E**mergency) before any particular contact does the trick!

Now would be a sensible time to ask for what we call a "tutorial" with a lecturer. Tutorials are shorter one to one sessions with a particular member of staff, and each lecturer will often have one set time period a week where tutorials can be booked. It's worth dropping an email to anyone who teaches a class that you might need a bit of support in, so that you can discuss things individually with them before the problem grows as more material is thrown at you. Even if you're not struggling with anything, it's sometimes nice to meet somebody properly so that they're easier to approach in future, should you need them.

Have a look around the Student Union – each university will have one! The Student Union will offer lots of different activity groups and societies that you're able to join, but they're also your first port of call if you have any other difficulties. These difficulties can be anything from an academic appeal and student finance problems to needing to complain about a member of staff. Sometimes they can even point you in the direction of finding a local job...or they may even employ you on a part time basis working for them. They are there to serve you and are always on your side.

So now that navigating the campus and the university routine doesn't seem so alien, it's a perfect chance to get involved in societies and other activities. I've seen societies ranging from arts and crafts, religious meetings, through to historic battle re-enactments! There will be something for everyone...and if you feel that a society is missing, you have the option to set one up! (More on how to go about doing that later!)

Get to know the university resources – I'll talk about what these might be in a bit more detail later, but now would be a good time to get to know the library, as well as any online resources that are available to you. Check in with how you submit your assignments online, so the process isn't stressful later on, and install your student email account on any smart phone/tablet you might have to make for easy access. Remember that many university resources/websites now have their own apps to make them even more accessible on the go!

One of my biggest regrets is not joining university societies. Not only are they great ways to stay entertained and look after your mental health, but they also enable you to mix with students on completely different courses who you might not have met otherwise. One thing I will say is that if you don't engage with a broader network of students, you may find that only spending time with the same group of people on your degree course will start to become difficult once you get into that second and third year. As a lecturer, I've noticed that it's always in the latter half of the second year that things can sometimes get a bit fractious between students (simply because
of the amount of time they spend with each other!) so it's brilliant to have this separate network to step away to for some breathing space if ever things get a little intense within your study group!

One last piece of advice for that second week...have your first night out! CELEBRATE! You have achieved something remarkable already. Be safe and sensible, but let your hair down – you've earned it.

<u>PARTY FEVER</u>

And this leads me on to my next little chapter; the "going out times" or "party fever" as I like to call it! For many a student, this is the first time that you have truly been away from home for any length of time, and of course that amount of independence is going to be as exciting as it might be daunting. Without the daily questions of "where are you going?" or "where have you been" it's all too tempting to go everywhere and do everything. Now, I'm not here to advise you against this – on the contrary, I encourage you to go out and let your hair down, however, all I ask of you is that you know your limits. Missing a lecture for the sake of a hangover is not worth doing - and trust me when I say that once you start missing lectures, it gets so much harder to get back on track. Not just in terms of work but also in terms of routine. The sooner you fall into a structure and get to grips with when you're in class, when you're at work, and when you have some time free, you will start to become far more productive and maximise how efficiently you can use your time – so ultimately, when you're "out, out" you'll enjoy it far more!

Now, you might hear it said that in your first year of study, you "only need 40%"
Let me break this down for you:

Each module that you study will be marked as per its own criteria. These marks will then be averaged to form your overall percentage mark for that module. However, it's not always a simple "average." In some cases, assignments are "weighted" differently. For example, one main project within the module might be worth 80% of the module mark, while another supplementary piece of work may only be worth 20%

As you move further through your degree, these final percentages will then themselves be averaged to determine your degree classification (first class, upper second class, second class, third class, fail) Now, for many universities, your first year of study does not officially count towards this final classification. Whilst there may of course be exceptions to this, it's generally the case that the only criteria for moving on to your next year of study is "passing" your first year; and for the most part, the pass mark is 40%.

Some universities are stricter about this than others, and of course I can only speak from my own personal experience, however; if in the first year, one module has gone a bit array for a student leaving them with a mark of 39% whilst the others remain well above the 40% pass mark, the university is often happy to allow you to progress, sometimes with the condition that you retake and pass the module, and sometimes not. As you can imagine, this can often lead to a bit of complacency amongst students — and many people feel that they don't have to apply themselves as much as they can (and should!) in their first year of study. I know, because the thought crossed my mind as a student! The first year of university study is stressful enough without the added worry of your academic achievement already having an impact on your final mark – and this is why the safety net of the 40% pass exists – but this safety net is also dangerous if you fall into its trap.

As I have said before when talking about enrolling and settling in, the best thing to establish is a routine, which will then encourage greater balance in all aspects of your university experience. If you set the precedent early on that "40% is the aim" then it'll be very hard to suddenly break this and switch into the "now I have to actually try" mind-set. When I'm marking assessments from a student in first year, it's eminently clear whether that person has potential, but what sadly seems to be the trend is that student settling into a particular 10% parameter (40-50%) as a result of a rehearsed way of learning. In reality, their marks could have been much better.

It's also worth remembering that staff members can look back on your past marks to get an overall picture of your learning and development – and you wouldn't want to disadvantage their perception of you in any way.

Where GCSE or A level study requires you to identify an argument or point relating to a particular issue, degree study requires you to expand upon that area with references to existing critique – and this is an art that cannot be perfected overnight. I strongly advise you to start writing in this way as soon as you possibly can. Often the mark schemes of first year modules are not as challenging as final year modules, so use the opportunity to learn and make mistakes while it won't negatively affect your overall classification!

<u>Do not let the 40% pass mark become a mantra!</u>

It is there to be a safety net in difficult times, and is not designed to be the limit of your capability.

So, back to the subject of "party fever"

Go out, have fun, mix with a wider network of people outside of those in your class or the other students in your flat – these are often the people who will become your lifelong friends, but remember that your priorities WILL CHANGE!

Make sure that you always remain mindful of the reason why you chose to attend university: yes, moving away and becoming independent is a massive benefit – but the reason is ultimately to GET A DEGREE.

My insight as a student and a lecturer is this:

In days gone by, it was rare for a member of the family to go to university. Those with bachelor's degrees were at the top of their profession, and professors seemed like fictional superheroes with bionic arms or something like that! Nowadays, more and more people are attending university, so much so that it has become the norm. In fact, many jobs now require a bachelor's degree as part of the basic employment criteria. This is of course fantastic that society has enabled a far greater range of people to receive an advanced education, but the knock-on effect of this is a reduced level of "specialism" for each bachelor's degree. In order to truly "excel" and get that interview for that dream job, you have to be aiming for those top classifications (first and upper second-class degrees) and your first year is the best opportunity to put yourself in the position to achieve this. Learn the style of writing required, focus the academic theory, refine your schedule and management of time – and then go out and party! This is the year to make mistakes, but also the year to pave the way for future success.

You don't need me to act like a nagging mother and remind you to be safe and responsible – but as with everything in life, balance and moderation is key. Establish your routine and reap the rewards later on.

Oh, and mine's a pina colada please!

UNDERSTANDING THE RESOURCES

When delivering a lecture, I use this phrase a lot "I'll put the work up on blackboard"

"What on earth is blackboard?!" is the question that goes through every first-year student's mind for at least the first month of study! "I thought they were those things in Victorian classrooms..."

Well yes, they are – but Blackboard is also this somewhat magical platform on which most universities host their learning materials. There are of course alternatives (Moodle/Brightspace/or another form of virtual learning environment) but Blackboard is the platform I am most familiar with, and seems the most commonly used across the institutions I have worked within.

So, what exactly is it?

Think of it like Facebook, Twitter and OneDrive all rolled into one, but with the dialogue being strictly university related as opposed to "#SundayBrunch" (which is currently the top UK trend on Twitter as I write this!)

On blackboard, each module that you're studying within your course will have its own page. This page will be run by your module tutor and module leader – so, as a student, you will have access to several separate course pages on blackboard at any one time.

The main functions of blackboard are as follows:

- Announcements can be posted by the module tutor, such as room changes, requirements for the next session, changes to timings or tutorials etc.

- It is a centralised database of all your learning materials for that particular module. You will/should be able to access digital copies of the module study guide, reading list, any specialised learning materials etc.
- Lecturers will be able to upload presentations or documents from sessions to enable home study.
  Not many lecturers will do this in advance of a session – we much prefer to deliver new content ourselves to ensure it is understood. After a session, we may want to upload the presentation we've put together to the module's blackboard page so that you can go over it at home in your own time.

For the reasons listed above, it's very important that you keep on top of your blackboard account. In my first year of my bachelor's degree, I was guilty of having the "I don't need it" mind-set – and whilst social media groups can keep you appraised of room changes, and your "in-class" notes may be comprehensive enough for you to not need to refer back to the original presentation, it is far better not to be reliant on this. Even if you never need to use any of the material, I strongly advise you to know where it is and how to access it...it may just come in handy later when you lose that one hand-out that you'd planned to reference from in your essay!

The other fundamental resource that will be centralised within your university is the library. Whilst I'm sure you don't need me to tell you what can be found in a library, I just thought I'd draw your attention to some other ways in which the library as a study resource can be helpful. Aside from having enough books to sink a ship, for most universities the library will also be the place where plenty of other study tools are hosted. Every university that I have attended and worked within was signed up to an institutional membership of various different digital platforms. This meant that anyone affiliated to the institution, namely staff and students, could have access to these resources, which include:

- Reference journals not available anywhere else
- Specialist academic papers, again not available anywhere else
- Specialised referencing tools (which can generate your in-text citations and references for you)
- And sometimes even software! (Microsoft office/audio & video editing software etc.)

So, do make use of it! As a lecturer, when I set an essay it is very common that the same articles, books and other sources are referenced between students. Whilst this is to be expected some of the time, it is SO refreshing when somebody takes the time to look at the peer review academic journals and other specialised resources that are available. This is the mark of somebody who is serious about their studies and wants to make a big impact on their chosen field. This is the person who gets the high marks — and because of their use of the resources available, they achieve these marks much more easily.

If in doubt, ask. Most, if not all universities will have a designated librarian employed to co-ordinate the university resources and answer any of your questions. They are the "reference gurus" and can be your secret weapon to success! Whenever I put together any module study guide, I am always sure to include the email address of the appropriate librarian who will be able to guide the students towards resources that will make completing the assignment a hell of a lot easier.

I guess the takeaway from this little section is; don't waste needless time floating around looking for inspiration. Use the resources available to you – I guarantee, you will miss them when they're gone.

It may also be the case that you find other online sources, such as referencing and citation tools, that you much prefer to the ones the university has available. This is exactly what happened to me! I couldn't get to grips with the ones the university signed up for, but I found this website "Neil's Toolbox" that did all my referencing for me…and good old Neil became my best friend for the whole of my degree!

If you do come across a tool that you find more effective but needs to be subscribed to, the librarian is the person you would talk to. They are often able and very happy to sign up to new services as they arrive, and make them available to you at the expense of the university as opposed to yourself!

So…use the force!
Or should I say – use the resources!

THE FIRST MARK ON THE PAPER

And then that dreaded day will come — the first exam, the first performance, the first exhibition or deadline...whatever it is — it'll come. AND YOU WILL BE READY!

Honestly, I loved it — and I was SO glad when it finally happened. Thinking back on how it went for me, I actually remember having my first two "assessments" in one day. One was a concert, where we had to perform a piece which we were then graded on, and the other was a theory exam. Both of these happened in week 7 of the first semester (which is often when the first assessment point will occur) Whilst I was quite possibly the most nervous I've ever been, I realised that in a way I was kind of relieved. I was relieved to finally have that first mark on the paper — that first grade. It didn't really matter what it was — what it meant was that I now had something to show for the seven weeks I was struggling to fit in and getting lost and learning this new way to live and work. Up until that moment, it felt as if walking away meant that I had achieved absolutely nothing, but week 7 allowed me to make that first mark on the degree — to make that first chip into the block of study that it would take me three years to break down. It really was a fantastic feeling — and I remember thinking this so clearly as I walked away from campus to Ealing Broadway station.

Of course, you're going to feel nervous, and that's completely natural and normal. As a lecturer, the first assessment is quite exciting for us. It's the first time that we really get to know a particular year group — we get to establish what their strengths are and the dynamic of how new social and working groups are forming. What we also get to establish, rightly or wrongly, is who are going to be the high achievers and who is going to need a little bit of extra encouragement.

Now for a bit of tough love: Part of the reason we lecturers have chosen to work in a university as opposed to a college or a school is because we want to work with adults. We want to work with adults who are passionate about our particular field of study, and we want to form working relationships with students who will ultimately help us further the knowledge we have about our chosen field. We are educating and building relationships with individuals who are our colleagues in our field of study, and who we hope will one day become our academic peers. With this in mind, there is the basic expectation that you take charge of your own learning. If things go wrong, we are more than happy to help you — but whereas in school, when you will be told by a teacher when things aren't up to scratch, we won't come looking for you.

We aren't expecting every piece of work to be first class, especially not straight away, but that first assignment is our chance to get to know how you work.

In the case of some students I have worked with, the first assignment highlighted that they were far better at speaking their answers (as I had discovered in class) than they were at writing them down. Their writing showed that they had brilliant ideas on the topic, but it was a little disjointed and lacked general flow. The student booked a tutorial with me to discuss their struggles, and I was able to point them in the direction of a writing support class run by the student services team. The next assignment they submitted scored 74% - which is in the "first class" grade boundary.

I suppose what I'm trying to say is that, taking everything into account, that first assignment is less about the actual exam and grade themselves, but instead more focused on the change of mental headspace that occurs once you've completed it. This is the same for both student and teacher.

This is your first big academic hurdle, but coming from someone who has sat both behind and in front of the lectern, you've got to see this as your passport onto the next stage as opposed to a wall being put down in your way. This is an exciting time to make your first impression — and once you've completed it, you'll never have to go through that "first exam anxiety" again.

After all, you know what they say: The journey of a thousand miles begins with one single step!

UNDERSTANDING MARKING AND GRADING

The university grading systems may be a little different to what you're typically used to. As previously mentioned, 40% is generally the pass mark for any university level piece of work. The grading will then be broken down into sections of 10% which are labelled as different classifications. The grades and boundaries are as follows:

40-49%: Pass (third class/3rd)
50-59%: Pass (second class/2:2)
60-69%: Pass (upper second class/2:1)
70% and above: Pass (first class/1st)

Sometimes universities will break down each category into subdivisions. Though this is more common for the upper end of the marking scale (i.e. having an "upper first" level for marks that are 80+), I have seen it done that each classification has a low, middle and high ranking, so you are greater able to understand a mark of 64% for example.

Then of course there is the practice of academic weighting. An example of this is:

One module has two assignments associated with it:
Assignment 1: Produce a portfolio of work with five original compositions based on a chosen theme. (80%)
Assignment 2: Produce a 2,000-word essay on your personal development, encompassing references to the work of practitioners and theory that has been applicable to your work. (20%)

Here, we see that one module is worth 80% of the overall module grade, while the other is worth 20%. Let me show you how this could impact the overall module grade if different results are achieved:

Assignment 1: 78%
Assignment 2: 51%

In this case, a student has received a very strong mark in their portfolio assignment, but the result is not quite as high for the essay.

The overall module grade would be 72.6% (rounded up to 73%) because the student has achieved a strong mark in the subject that is weighted more heavily.

Flip this around in terms of assignment weighting, and the overall module grade would be 56.4% (rounded down to 56%)
This results in a drop of two classifications!

Whilst you should always strive to achieve the highest marks you can in any and all assignments you submit, it's worth remaining mindful of which ones will have a greater bearing on your overall classification (for both the particular module and the degree as a whole.) You can use any simple "module grade calculator" online to assist with this. Try not to become reliant on forecasting exactly what you need to achieve, as this could lead to increased anxiety – but always check in!

It is my firm belief that, as an educator, the full scope of the mark scheme should be used (i.e. if something is worth 85%, or indeed 15%, it should be marked as such) I have seen several occasions where mid-range marks have been adopted, when they could have perhaps been a little more extreme. Whilst I'm really pleased to say that every lecturer training course I have attended over the past year has stressed the need to use the full range of marks available, I am aware that it is not an encouraged practice everywhere. Whilst I don't really want to get into the politics of this (not least, because it'll become something of a rant, when I'd much rather talk about cheerier topics such as your inevitable university success) it is important to remain mindful that this is the case. Marks above 75% often have to be defended by lecturers to in-house and external academic quality regulators — so, even if a lecturer wants to be a bit more lenient, the extra need for justification means that it's not always possible. That being said, there have of course been cases where work has been under-marked, and my advice is this:

You will know, in your heart of hearts, what mark your work truly deserves. If you ask yourself truthfully whether you could have put a few more hours in, and the answer is yes, my advice is to trust in your lecturers and accept the mark you have been given — as difficult as this may be. There may well be options to retake the module, or indeed mitigate if you have mitigating circumstances (I'll talk more about this later.)

However, there are some cases (albeit rarer) where you may well have been under-marked. Everyone's human, and we all make mistakes — it happens.
If this is the case, you might want to consider launching an "academic appeal" Usually it is the student union that will help with this. Sometimes a student services team or "one stop shop" might be able to advise you on how to open one of these cases.

The process for this is typically as follows:
You would be required to submit your appeal generally within fourteen days of receiving your confirmed mark. Appeals will almost always be submitted to the student union's academic advice officer — but the union will be able

to point you in the right direction if this is not the case for your particular institution.

You will most likely have a meeting with the academic advice officer, and they will explain the grounds of appeal open to you, which usually are:

- Procedural error – where you think your marks have been added up incorrectly.
- Extenuating circumstances – essentially good reasons why you might not have been able to achieve your potential.

NB: These would usually have been submitted as "mitigating circumstances" earlier on – but you are still able to submit them afterwards (backdated) if there is a good reason!

You will then collate your appeal (the SU will be able to guide you on this.) Be sure to be very clear about the reasons for your appeal (including which ground you are appealing on, be it procedural or under extenuating circumstances), and provide evidence as required. This may be in the form of doctor's notes or other official documents. Your case will be reviewed by a caseworker and the chairperson of your university's academic appeals panel. This will usual be via email or call – it's not very common that an official face-to-face panel meeting is arranged to hear a specific appeal case. In most cases, the outcome of the academic appeal can be determined remotely.

Most universities try to ensure that the appeals process does not extend beyond a period of three months. (Not least because this avoids elongated impact on your wellbeing and your future studies.)

Your student union representative will be able to talk you through your case notes and ultimate outcome of the appeal. It's worth remembering that not all appeals are successful, and in the long-term it is far easier to seek mitigation (which could involve an extension) prior to sitting an exam or submitting an assessment than it is to attempt to change the result via the method of appeal later. I think it's better that you hear it from me: the harsh reality is that not many academic appeals are successful. Going back to what I said earlier about the need to take charge of your own learning, most forms of mitigation are granted prior to any exam or submission so any adjustments can be made. The good news is that these adjustments often mean that an appeal is not necessary because the student has been successful. Hopefully, you'll never need to get to the stage of submitting an academic appeal but nevertheless, it's important to be aware of what you're entitled to and where you can go for support. You shouldn't feel any shame in submitting an appeal – the process exists because there is sometimes a genuine need for them!

By the time you have submitted a couple of assessments and sat a few exams, you will fully understand the grading process. I once had a very wise teacher who said to me:

"If you read the mark scheme, you can decide yourself what mark you want to get"

And these words are so true! If you haven't been given a mark scheme for your assignment (though they should be available in any module study guide or other course literature), refer back to the module's original learning objectives and be sure to meet every single one of them. Do not omit any information, and follow each objective or piece of marking criteria like a to-do list. If you provide absolutely everything that is asked of you, you broaden the possibilities of examiners finding valid points to award marks for!

I'm sure you will all have very successful university journeys ahead, and I hope this chapter helped you understand a little bit more about those dreaded percentages! Sometimes it feels so counterintuitive to have to put a number to a piece of work — particularly in creative subjects like art or music, where most things are subjective to a degree. This number is by no means a measure of your potential, creativity or ability to excel both later on in your studies and in your professional lives. Just as you might feel you have to jump through hoops in creating pieces of work that fit marking criteria (and I felt this way a lot!), this is a hoop that we have to jump through to ensure that the university complies with academic standards. This safeguards the credibility of your degree and keeps the industry as professional as it can be. The high marks are always there for the taking — and they are always achievable!

MEET YOUR LECTURER

I'VE GOT PROBLEMS WITH MY LECTURER
WHAT TO DO WHEN IT'S GONE A BIT FURTHER THAN A
MILD DISLIKE!

As much as we all like to be liked, sometimes it just doesn't happen. Whilst I like to think that all lecturers are supportive and nurturing of their students, just as with all people, sometimes you might find that isn't the case. As a student, I had one or two lecturers who made my blood boil, so I know just how tricky it can be when you have to be so reliant on somebody with whom you don't quite see eye to eye. Honestly, this lecturer (and I won't name any names) was a big of a dragon! I could go into details, but knowing my luck, they'll read this book and send me an email outlining all the places I went wrong...just as if I was back in second year! (Shudders!) Whilst it's not an excuse, some people don't realise the effect that their words have on others. I can think of one instance where I was in my second year of studies and I was singing a duet with someone in my class. Having a low voice, I always sing the bottom line – and our lecturer for that class turned to me and said, "I'm not going to work with you Madeline, because no one listens to the low part –

you're not the important one" These words made me feel really worthless and small, and while not a personal criticism, I felt very isolated in all of those classes. Sometimes, things just hurt — and it's important that you address them, and don't suffer alone.

Anyway, not having a positive working relationship with a lecturer can cause all sorts of worry; what if they give me a bad mark in my exam/assessment, what if don't get given any opportunities to showcase myself, what if I get picked on in a seminar today and I don't know the answer? All of these worries might sound silly when you think of them individually, but the stress and anxiety that comes with them can weigh a tonne. Here are a few things that might help if you find yourself in this situation:

<u>Ask a friend for their take on things</u>
This is not at all to say that the problem isn't real or substantial, but if you're a worrier like me, there's every chance that you might be viewing the situation as worse than it might actually be. The first step that I would advise you to take is to speak to a friend from that particular class and ask them for their take on things. Perhaps they might have noticed a negative dynamic, or might be feeling something similar — but if not, it's worth asking them to observe during the next lecture, with a view to giving an honest opinion afterwards. If it's just your perspective, then you can trust in their judgement and try to find a more positive mind-set when approaching the class, but if they do notice something negative, then you can follow the next steps.

<u>Make an appointment with your personal tutor/or course leader if your personal tutor is the cause of your concern</u>

Feel free to take someone with you to this appointment if the issue is difficult to discuss – just make sure that, out of courtesy, you advise the staff member that you will be bringing someone along when you book the appointment. Be sure to be open and honest about the magnitude of your concerns. If you feel that you are unable to continue in that class, then you must say so! Alternatively, if you have any suggestions that would make life easier (such as moving study groups so that you are working with peers you are more familiar with), then be sure to put this forward too. This meeting should be all about finding a solution that is in everybody's best interests. In my experience, it's far better to put everything out in the open at this first opportunity so you don't have to repeat yourself or confuse the situation by adding details later. If it helps you, make a few notes of what you want to say, giving dates and times of any incidents if applicable. In turn, be sure to jot down the responses from your staff member. (If you have brought anyone along to the meeting with you, you could consider asking them to do this for you) Nine times out of ten, the staff member will follow up your discussion with an email to outline any decisions made in writing, but it's worth keeping your own notes so you can query anything that isn't correct or add any missing details should you need to later on.

<u>Check in with the student union</u>

This is one of the key reasons the student union exists! An important thing to say here is that the student union can always act and liaise on your behalf should you feel unable to instigate a discussion with a member of staff yourself. If you don't feel able to make an appointment and go through the meeting process outlined above, there is absolutely no shame in involving the student union — they will be very happy to help and support you. If you have already arranged a meeting with a member of staff, you could consider asking somebody from the student union to accompany you — if not, you've got the option of simply flagging the complaint with a member of union staff so they can follow up with you at a later date. Talking to the student union is a good idea — they might well point you in the direction of another member of staff/student who is able to provide support, or help you engage with some wellbeing activities to look after your mental and physical health. They can be involved as much as you would like them to!

If no satisfactory resolution is reached, you can escalate the issue to a member of senior staff. You can contact them yourself to arrange a meeting, or have a union representative do this for you. Whereas in previous meetings when an informal resolution was the objective, by this point, this will almost certainly constitute an official complaint against that particular member of staff. Do not take this lightly, but at the same time, do not be put off by the severity of the complaint if you have been mistreated or disadvantaged. You have to look after yourself and put your mental and physical health before anything else. If a complaint needs to be made, then the student union and appropriate members of staff will support you all the way through the process.

POSSIBLE OUTCOMES:

- A change of study group – Perhaps there could be an option to study exactly the same module, but with a different tutor?

- A change of module – If you are early enough on in the semester, and there is the option to select a different module, you may be offered this as a possible resolution.

- A meeting with the tutor (mediated with other members of staff) – If there are no logistical resolutions like the ones listed above, your personal tutor (or other staff member) may offer to set up a meeting with the lecturer in question to air any concerns and see if a resolution can be reached. This will only be arranged if you agree to it, and do not feel pressured into agreeing if you do not feel comfortable with the idea!

If the above is unsatisfactory:

- An internal investigation may be launched into your allegations against the staff member. This investigation may also be conducted by external third parties if it is deemed appropriate.

- If you are no longer comfortable with attending the university, the administrative team may help you to facilitate a transfer.

- If the investigating authority deems it appropriate, that

- staff member may be disciplined or dismissed accordingly.

But it's important to remember that these are on the more extreme end of the possible resolutions, and for the most part, a meeting with your personal tutor or other appropriate member off staff should resolve the issue in the best interests of everyone involved.

In short, always remember to look after yourself. Don't make issues bigger than they need to be, but at the same time, don't ignore problems if they arise. These things always work out better when they are addressed early – and there are plenty of university organisations to support and care for you every step of the way.

Of course, the likelihood is that once you settle into the swing of things, you'll relish being inspired by the likeminded people who act as your lecturers. Hopefully, you'll never need to use the information in this chapter – but just keep it in your back pocket just in case it can help you when you may need it!

I'VE GOT PROBLEMS WITH MY CLASSMATES WORKING WITH STUDENTS WHO AREN'T QUITE AS ENTHUSIASTIC AS YOU!

In the vast majority of cases, university will be an endless wave of enthusiasm from mixing with likeminded students with similar passions and ambitions – but whilst I don't mean to sound at all pessimistic (I'm sure this won't happen to you), sometimes things don't quite go to plan with our classmates.

I speak from experience here: I remember this one particular module that involved the two words I dreaded most...group work. Honestly, I couldn't stand it! I hated the idea that we would all be marked as one, regardless of the fact that one person had put all the work in, while the others simply turned up on the day. I was lucky that almost every one of my fellow students was fully committed to their studies, but there are of course times when group work doesn't go to plan. There was this one assignment where I knew nobody in the class, and eventually ended up in a group with four people who I didn't actually see in person again until the assessment day! I attempted to get in touch with them, but they seemed pretty difficult people to get hold of! Anyway, despite my wish to complete the assignment jointly, I ended up panicking to put together a presentation for us all to deliver on the day. It would have been much better if we had all put our heads together and used our different specialisms to create an exciting presentation, but this was the result of not addressing the problem early. As you can imagine, I was very angry and anxious about the situation, but angrier with myself for not doing anything about it. If I'm honest with you, I got to the point where I really resented working hard. I had no incentive or enthusiasm to turn up to that particular module's classes, and in the lectures, I would often find myself zoning out and seeing how long I could nurse a tube of fruit pastels rather than actually concentrating!

Now that I find myself taking the classes as opposed to sitting in them, I have lot of sympathy for students in this position – and believe me when I say that most, if not all, lecturers (certainly at my place of work) feel the same. Here are some of my top tips if you find yourself facing the issue of troublesome classmates:

Talk to them (but only if you can) – If your dynamic is such that you feel able to say "guys, you really need to pull your socks up here", then of course this is the logical first step. Sometimes it helps to address this as more of a group problem by saying "we really need to pull our socks up", and whilst this may seem unfair to include yourself in this statement (and it is!), just keep in mind that it might just be easier for them to take than a full-on telling off! Only take this step if you feel able. Don't put yourself at any risk of being further isolated or unhappy.

Tell your lecturer – PLEASE don't feel like you're snitching if you have to take the issue to your lecturer. I stress that none of this is your fault, and you cannot be at all criticised for wanting the best mark possible for your degree. This is your tuition that you're paying for, and it's not fair to have it jeopardised by people who don't care quite as much about success. Be sure to be open and honest with your lecturer. If you feel that having them speak to the group will assist, then ask for this. If not, then tell them that you feel it may sour the dynamic – they will be sensitive to this. More often than not, your lecturer will ask if you feel able to continue working with the group you're in...and you must answer them honestly!

POSSIBLE SOLUTIONS

(Whilst your lecturer will probably suggest all of these possible solutions to you, it might be worth checking out the list below to see if you can suggest any alternatives. This will make it seem as though you've really thought about ways to resolve the situation, and you're far more likely to have allowances made
in your favour! I have suggested some of the below to my own students who have had group assignment related issues:

- Change groups (goes without saying really) – but make sure you don't make it seem like you only want to change groups to be with your friends! Stress that the issue is not the people themselves, but more the fact that the assignment workload hasn't been shared.

- Be marked separately to other members of your group – Perhaps you and your lecturer can make some sort of arrangement that enables you to be marked separately based on the work that you have completed, meaning that not all members of the group achieve the same overall mark for the module.

- Adapt the assignment so that you are able to submit it as an individual – In some cases a group assignment can be adapted so that it can become an individual piece of work. If you are really struggling with your group dynamic and share of the workload, perhaps this is something you could suggest as a solution to your lecturer?

- Carry on as normal, but inform the lecturer of the circumstances — Sometimes it's simplest and least disruptive to carry on as normal, but if you inform your lecturer of the situation, they will ensure that no unfair marks are awarded and each group member's contribution to the overall assignment is marked accordingly.

Speaking from experience, the worst thing you can do in this situation is to let your anger and stress fester and go unresolved. This can lead to much larger arguments and disputes later down the line, and could also result in you (and indeed your classmates) receiving marks that aren't fair. As lecturers, we always try to spot where this might be happening and intervene accordingly, but unfortunately, we can miss things, and it's really important that you bring any struggles that you have of this nature to attention. In my case, I did end up dropping my lecturer and email (though much later than I should have done), and making them aware of the uneven distribution of the workload was enough for me to feel much less angry about the whole situation. Don't let a situation like this spoil your enthusiasm and enjoyment of the university experience — this is your degree and your education...no one else's!

SUMMER IS APPROACHING!

By the time those nights get shorter and you find yourself sitting outside at 7pm, noticing that daylight is still lingering, you will feel like a seasoned pro at this whole university thing — and you've earned that feeling! The winter is over, and now you get a chance to really stretch your legs and see what you can do. January will see the start to your "second semester" of university study. For some students, that will mean a complete new set of academic modules, and for others the previous modules will continue running (though often as a "part 2")

With each lecture, you will find yourself feeling more assured and more comfortable in your methods of study, and it's at this point that the phrase "I can't believe first year is nearly over" will cross your mind! You'll start to see feint, but certain glimpses of the cap and gown and the graduation ceremony as you inch ever closer to the moment when you can strut your stuff across that stage and collect your degree — and you will be amazed at how quickly that moment arrives! I know I'll just be one of the many people you hear say "time will fly by — it'll be over before you know it," but it really is true.

As it was for me as a student, this will probably be the first time you feel that palpable sense of optimism that YOU WILL GET THERE. For me, it was about March time that I first pinpointed the moment when I stopped feeling convinced that I was never going to see the end. Instead my thoughts shifted to "you've already done one semester, you can't waste it now" which, on reflection, is probably on the more pessimistic end of the forward-thinking spectrum! (We'll leave that there!)

You'll be amazed that, as if by magic, you have more hours in the day. You'll feel fresher, and energised, and less concerned by those small teething issues that drove you mad in the first semester. By now, you'll feel comfortable in the company of your lecturers and fellow students alike, and they too will be starting to get to grips with the way you work, what makes you tick, and how you're settling in. This does come with a small warning though:

As I found during my first year of university study, the first summer holiday milestone seemed in itself the end of the degree. I had a very much "get to May and then you can forget about it for the next four months mind-set" which, before I go any further, is not a bad thing! It is totally and completely expected for you to rejoice the end of studies, at least for a few months. We staff members would be lying if we said we didn't expect you to go out and party with your friends with absolutely no intention of logging on to blackboard or hitting the books – but do try your best not to abandon it completely.

Though some might disagree with me, my advice to you when approaching your summer holidays (and you only get two of them in a 3-year degree) is this:

Try to think ahead to your long-term ambitions and what you can do to facilitate them happening. What I mean by this is, a lot of people finish their degree and then immediately find themselves stuck and having to "start from zero" in terms of taking steps to achieve their desired ambitions. What you really want to be doing is hitting the ground running as soon as those final university moments are over! If you know that the job you want to do will require a portfolio, use the summer to start building it. If your job will require interviews, then start to construct your CV so you can build upon it later. If you are a performer and are intending on auditioning, then make a show-reel or a voice-reel. Artists...draw and paint! Writers...write! You get my drift. You can then get opinions from lecturers and fellow students to help make these materials even better. I always liked to see the summer as "bonus time" – essentially, time where you can still live off of student finance, or stay in the city, but without the stress of attending lectures and writing essays. Even if you use the summer to work to save up some funds to support you later, this is all time well spent! What I'm saying is: try to see the summer break as the clock slowing, as opposed to stopping completely. Time is still passing, and the new term will come around again – but enjoy the calm, and enjoy the freedom to diversify your activities, which actively forge the building blocks for your future career and success!

LOSING FOCUS

As with anything; the longer you do it, the more likely it is to start to feel like a chore, and returning to study after a period of time away is no exception. On a more positive note, settling back into second year seemed like a walk in the park when compared with the jarring start to the university experience. I remember walking through waves of new entrants struggling to read the campus maps and enjoying the reminder of how far I'd come in just one short year. Remembering how I felt so helpless, it was great to be able to help others — and perhaps you might even consider volunteering to become a student ambassador to help ease the transition of others into the university environment. If this is something you're interested in, your student services team or student union will be all too happy to assist you!

Another part of my jump back into second-year university study that I remember very well was the distinct inability to concentrate or focus on anything. I refer to this time as my "cardigan phase" when all I seemed to wear was the same Primark cardigan in different colours for a period of about three months! The funny thing is, I don't even remember buying said cardigans – they just seemed to materialise! Instead of focusing on studying or socialising, I found myself wanting to head to bed at 8:30, drink hot chocolate and altogether turn into my Grandma. Then again, the start of second year is a strange time...

From my personal experience, there was quite a big change in the style of university lectures delivered when I started my second year of study. Lectures changed from each class being delivered by the same one or two members of staff, to having a much more expansive range of lecturers, each a specialist in their own area. This style is now much more the norm when compared to the "one size fits all" approach that had been adopted previously. Going from having one or two lecturers to liaise with to a completely different point of contact for each separate module was particularly challenging, and meant that I did lose focus somewhat for the beginning of the autumn semester. Given that this diverse mode of study is now by far the most common, I will share with you some insights on how you're able to combat that frustrating inability to focus – both from where I went wrong as a student and from what I am now learning from my students:

Follow your daily routine and stick to it – including the good bits!
The temptation for any kind of routine is firstly to disregard it completely! This starts with an "I'll do that bit tomorrow" mind-set, but before you know it, tomorrow's backlog expands a month! The next stage of this is to ban any kind of social contact and remotely fun activity until said tasks are completed. I've been there and done this – and I've seen

students go there and do this...and believe me, the end result is feeling much more stressed and producing a quality of work that is far below what you could achieve. You need to work hard, but you also need to play hard – and whether playing hard is having a loud and enthusiastic party, or lying in bed and watching bad TV with a chocolate milkshake – it needs to be done just as much as the studying. The fact of the matter is; everybody needs that basic level of escapism. I've been known to flick through the news or watch the odd YouTube video between teaching classes – and I'm not about to stop any time soon. It is unrealistic of any lecturer to expect you not to have this balance...but that's the key...balance!

<u>Invest in a BEAUTIFUL notebook</u>

I don't know about you, but I'm one of these people that absolutely ADORES a beautifully handwritten piece of paper – and a whole book full of beautiful notes literally makes my mouth water! I was always one of those people who would rip out a page if ever I made one mistake and rewrite the whole thing so it looked perfect. Now, I'm not saying to go to that extent by any means, but there's a lot to be said for a beautiful notebook. It doesn't need to be expensive or flash – what I mean is, if you have a lovely place to keep your notes (and you keep it lovely) you're more inclined to a) write more and b) focus more when you're writing it. It's kind of a win-win situation...and the by-products are a gorgeous set of notes to revise from, and a greater understanding of the lecture or topic as a whole! Trust me, it works!

To-do lists

Those of you that know me will know how much of a big "lister" I am! There's no feeling that is more satisfying than crossing off a task, or putting a giant tick next to a completed job. Having a to-do list gives you focus to your efforts. You can make daily ones to concentrate a period of time, or your lists can be broader and further reaching. The key to success with to-do lists is to keep them reasonable. Don't put something monumental down like "get a new job" or "buy a house" amongst your "send this email to Joe Bloggs" level tasks – that just means that you're denying yourself that sense of final completion. By all means make lists with broad ambitions, but make these your "goals for the 6 months/year(s)" which are not to be placed amongst your standard day-to-day tasks.

Get a big red pen to cross off those outstanding bits and pieces, and you won't be able to stop...it's addictive!

Set time goals

This is something I love to do whenever I'm teaching a class that's perhaps losing a little focus or enthusiasm (particularly the 4pm on Friday lecture, as you can imagine!) When things are becoming a bit more difficult to focus on, give yourself a challenge – you will thrive on it. Say to yourself, as I say to my classes:

"Right, it's 4pm now. By 5pm I'll have done x, y and z...and then I'll stop"

That gives you a concentrated time window to achieve something that allows you a blast of effort as well as a definitive end time. End times are great resources to help you focus. There's something very empowering about having a "this will be done in two hours because I'm not going to let it extend past then" mind-set. It gives you peace of mind knowing that something WILL be finished — you just haven't quite got there yet.

Try it — it may completely change the way you work.

If all else fails...stop, sleep and repeat

It's ok to have an off day. Everyone has to have one once in a while — even just so they can greater appreciate it when they're on top form!

For whatever reason your mind is wondering; stress, illness, tension, tiredness — it's ok! Sometimes your brain reaches "saturation point" when you simply cannot take any more information in. You're like a sponge so soaked up with water that you can't absorb anymore! It's very obvious when any class I teach has reached this stage; they get fidgety and uncomfortable and there will probably be a few more audible moans and groans than those usually present! Sometimes, the time is right to step away — after all, persisting in a negative mind-set can be just as bad as not persisting at all. If this is the case, and you feel fidgety and uncomfortable and so stressed and wound up that it feels as though you're about to explode, (we've all been there!) take yourself away, eat well, zone out (rubbish TV is calling!) and have a good sleep. You can repeat anything you've missed tomorrow by consulting the learning resources available, including the lecturers themselves. Don't worry about asking for help, I've had students come to me expressing similar problems, and the conversation went something like this:

STUDENT: Madeline, is there any chance you could explain *that* part of yesterday's lecture — I just couldn't take it in yesterday.

MADELINE: Sure, no problem. Yes, I did notice that everyone was a bit flat yesterday. It's such a busy time, I know everyone must be feeling a bit drained.

(Explains work)

Would it help if you booked a tutorial for a bit of extra support?

STUDENT: Actually, that would be great.

(Books tutorial)

MADELINE: Feel a bit better?

STUDENT: Loads. Sorry, about that — I just kind of zoned out yesterday.

MADELINE: Don't stress! I know you're usually on fantastic form, and thank you so much for coming to see me.

So, lecturers WANT to help you — and, letting you in on a little secret, it makes you look better if you admit your problems.

It makes you seem professional, open and honest and ultimately somebody that staff member would want to work with in the future - I was taught by many members of staff who later became my colleagues!

So, stop, sleep and repeat — and you will feel all the better for it.

ACADEMIC SUPPORT
HELP! I'VE FORGOTTEN HOW TO WRITE MY NAME – LET ALONE WRITE AN ESSAY!

As you progress through your degree, there is no question that the work will get harder. Ideally, this increased difficulty is in proportion to your improvement in academic standard and you won't particularly notice the work is any harder – but sometimes it doesn't quite turn out this way.

All lecturers should follow the learning path set out in the module study guide or equivalent handbook document, and the transition from easy to more challenging work should be graduated equally over your years of study. However, there are some cases when a bigger jump is required. I remember this one class called "orchestration and arranging" which I took as an option in my second year. It started off relatively easy (well, I say easy – I'd never have been able to do it as a first-year), but then we were set this one assignment and HOLY MACARONI! I have never attempted anything quite so hard in all my life. We had to orchestrate this one piece of music in a particular style and honestly, my work looked like a giant spider had jumped into a pot of black ink, and then proceeded to walk across my paper in any random direction. It was honestly horrific. Then I was asked to write essays, and then reports, and then dissertations – and I had no idea what the difference was! It took me spelling my name wrong to realise that I needed to go back to basics and refresh my fundamental understanding of academic literature.

Let me share some insights with you, from both a student and a lecturer perspective:

Essay: An essay is a (generally short) piece of academic writing about a particular subject. Most academic essays should be written in "third person" unless otherwise stipulated (so no "I did this, I did that or "from my perspective.") The exception to this may be a piece of critical writing about your personal development, or something similar. In either case, your writing should be backed up by references to existing literature that strengthens your overall points or argument.

This leads me on to:

References: References are what they say on the tin... "references" to existing literature. When you quote an academic professional, whose findings support the points you are attempting to make, this is a reference. For some referencing methods, you will use what we call an "in-text citation" to pinpoint whose words you're using, and this will then be backed up with a full list of references later on.

There are several different systems of referencing, which are contrasting ways of presenting the same material. You might come across the Harvard, APA, and MLA methods — and maybe even more! Generally, your university will make it known to you which style of referencing they use institutionally, however some may be happy for you to choose your preferred method as long as it is used consistently. I've always worked with the Harvard method, and I'll demonstrate it a little bit below.

If I wanted to reference something I've said in this book...let's use the first line of this explanation as an example of the quote I want to use: 'References are what they say on the tin' - Not very informative, I know — but it does the job.

I could say: When discussing referencing, lecturer Madeline Castrey said 'References are what they say on the tin' (Castrey, 2020) I found this to be a very informative insight...blah blah blah.

The first thing to note here is the use of quotation marks rather than speech marks. This may seem to go without saying, but you'd be surprised how often this mistake crops up!

The Harvard system (as outlined here), and indeed some others use "in-text citations" to credit the author in the body of the text, and direct the reader to the correct entry in the full reference list at the end of the work. A basic in-text citation in the Harvard style would include the author's surname, a comma, and the year of publication in brackets — in this case (Castrey, 2020)

Depending on the system you are using, and indeed the material you are referencing, some in-text citations may need to include page numbers or other information - BUT DON'T BE DAUNTED. Once you get into your stride, you won't even think about it. Just to put your mind at rest, I never needed to waver from this type of basic citation (and indeed full reference) through the whole of my bachelors and masters degrees...so the information included here may well be enough to see you through!

In the reference list at the end of the piece (which would typically be sorted alphabetically), I would include the following full reference:

Castrey, M (2020). *Fresher Pressure*. London: Blossom Spring Publishing. 16.

Broken down as:
Surname, Initial (YEAR). *Book Title. (In italics) Publishing* location: Publisher. Page number (or range)

Websites are also a common thing that you may reference. In the Harvard system, you would cite this the same. Some websites may state an author, in which case the citation may still be (Castrey, 2020), though some may not – in which case, the name of the website will be sufficient for the in-text citation; (Castrey Website, 2020)

Your full reference might look something like this:
Castrey, M. (2020). *Fresher Pressure.* Available: www.fresherpressure.internet. Last accessed 17th May 2020.

Broken down as:
Surname, Initial (YEAR). *Website Title. (In italics)* Available: Full URL. Last accessed DATE YOU LAST VISITED THE WEBSITE.

There are small variations to this depending on whether there is a credited individual author or an "organisational author" (like BBC News for instance) but I won't bore you with those details here! There are many online resources that will quickly and simply clear this up for you, should you require a differentiation — and of course your lecturers will be more than happy to help you too!

Now, this is the Harvard way of referencing — there are plenty of others. Some will replace in-text citations with footnotes and endnotes, which use a numbering system to sort your references that will appear either at the bottom of the page on which they are written (footnotes) or at the end of piece of work (endnote.)
I would advise you to find out which system your university uses as soon as you can, and of course use the academic resources available to you (online reference generators etc.)

Reports: Reports are typically used to express and present the results of something (be it an experiment, a new way of working, or personal development) Whenever I set a report as an assignment, I expect there to be subheadings, diagrams, pictures, graphs and other appendices to help make points. It is still a formal academic piece of writing, and the appropriate referencing method still needs to be used.
Someone once asked me if a report could be described as a "pretty essay" — and essentially, this is true! They are often very helpful ways of presenting longer pieces of writing that would benefit from being broken down to a greater degree. I love a report myself! They always seemed much easier to write and much more satisfying to look at!
Dissertation: A dissertation is essentially a long essay on a particular subject, often presented as a "final" piece of academic writing for a degree or other qualification. Now, whilst the essay content of the dissertation will always

constitute the main part, it is true to say that to a small extent, a dissertation is a combination of an essay and a report. What I mean by this is, while some dissertations work much more effectively as a long single piece of prose, others will benefit from the inclusion of graphs, diagrams and other figures to assist in making points. As long as these are referenced correctly and are appropriate to your subject, they can be included. I have occasionally found it useful to include supporting material as an "appendix" i.e. a bit added onto the end.

For example, when referencing a piece of music, or a graph that is simply too big to include in the main body of text, I could say "see appendix 1" Then, I would include whatever the data is at the end of the document, labelled "appendix 1"

It's simple really when you think about it, but when you're in the midst of a degree, it's all too easy to get swept up in the paranoia of academic achievement and lose sight of these basics. I hope that the above provides you with a little bit of "at a glance" assistance with these fundamentals, should you lose sight of them!

Now for some tips and pointers on how to improve your overall academic writing:

Always write to express your opinion

This might seem counter-intuitive given that lots of your academic writing will be in "third-person," but this tip has helped me endlessly. For whatever you're writing about, even if it's the most boring thing in the world to you, you should form an opinion. If that opinion is "this is totally irrelevant and pointless to my field of study" – then that's still a valid opinion that, if backed up by good literary and other academic sources, can still be a credible viewpoint!

Some assignments will really inspire you, and they can fire you up so much that you find yourself having to dramatically cut down your word count at the end of it. Others, will leave you wanting to write "I'm bored" 80 times in white text so submission software shows more words than there actually appear to be. (Don't go getting any ideas now!) Ironically, I found writing essays about my personal development, which should technically be the area I am most passionate about, the most tedious.

The best thing I can advise you to do is to research and explore the topic enough to allow you to find a particular area that really gets your thoughts racing. Then you'll find that the essay starts to write itself – and that writing comes across as passionate, enthusiastic and knowledgeable, and will receive a much higher mark for it!

<u>Shake things up a bit!</u>
Perhaps you might have noticed this from reading this book, but just in case you haven't, I write VERY long sentences! I always have done, and I just can't help myself. Not anymore.

See – that short sentence of just two words there was quite effective, wasn't it?!

Always keep the reader on their toes. Just think of how many hundreds of essays lecturers read year on year. Be the one they remember!

- Change your sentence structure

- Use a full and diverse range of punctuation — correctly of course!
- Use expansive vocabulary
- Use industry standard terminology if applicable.

We will thank you for it with a lovely high mark!

"Out of order" can be a good thing!

It can be very demanding to write things in the order that they will appear in your essay. Sometimes you're really not feeling penning an introduction, or breaking down your full range of methodology — and other times, that's the bit you want to get done! I used to write in chronological order, but when I gave myself the permission to break this, my quality of academic writing greatly improved. It can be a very worthwhile activity to write a short section of any assignment when inspiration suddenly strikes. All the more satisfying is watching a big jump in the word count when you paste this new section into the main body of your work. Whilst you have to be careful to avoid your writing becoming convoluted (sometimes you can end up waffling if you "re-make" points in different sections), writing out of order can be a tactical way of completing any academic writing to a high standard. As long as you stick to the main sections of your work to avoid any repetitions and ambiguity, you could just change the way you write!

Have a designated writing place and time

Referring back to my notes about how to overcome the occasional loss of focus, I have found that having a writing place and time can really help me to become more productive — ultimately enabling you to write more, in less time!

We've all gone to "work in bed" with our laptop perched on top of our duvet, Netflix open on one internet search window while we "research" on the other one. Believe me – we've all been there, myself included (and far more often than you might think!) Whilst this might indeed be the comfiest way of writing an essay, and you will eventually get it done, you'll find that it takes double or maybe even triple the time to finish it. Find a place, it could be at your kitchen table or in the university library, or maybe a spot in a local coffee shop, to mark as your "writing zone." Whenever you're in this place, you are dedicated to your writing. You will then start to mentally and physically attribute this place to efficient and productive working, and you'll make that mental connection to your work with much more ease going forwards. It can even help to put a time window on this:

Wednesdays from 2pm-4:30pm – writing in the library.

This then forms part of your weekly schedule and broader routine, and allocates that set time in the week to be productive. Once you get used to that time slot, you'll even start to prepare for it, both consciously and subconsciously. You'll pack your notebook and pencil case the night before, and you may well sleep more deeply in preparation for the day ahead.

I have always found this useful, and I continue to incorporate it into my weekly schedule. Even if I don't have any direct written assignments to complete, that slot can always be converted into "life admin" or any kind of task that might feel mundane and elongated. That way, all of that tedium is concentrated within that one period of time, leaving you more free and flexible on other days!

<u>Think about writing how you speak!</u>

We all know how to speak! We are all fantastic improvisers – rarely ever knowing or planning what we're going to say next, and yet always finding a way to formulate and deliver coherent sentences that make our point and send a loud and clear message of what our intentions are...Isn't this the main aim of essay writing?!

"I'd never thought of it like that!" I hear you say...

Well, it's true! There's a definite and concrete link here.

If ever I ask any students to explain the answer to a question or to clarify what they mean in something they have written, I always get a coherent answer. I listen as they formulate their argument clearly and concisely – without the need to consult any learning materials or revision notes, and my reply is ALWAYS: "Fab. Write that down." The fact of the matter is that we are all able to make our intentions clear – it is how we survive. Therefore, if we "write how we speak" the points we make should always be clear and concise.

I appreciate things get tricky when you throw in the need for full and complete academic referencing, and the inclusions of introductions and explanations of methodology that would not normally feature in our day-to-day conversations and vocabulary. I completely understand that. However, if you can enter into the mind-set of writing in the same way you would speak, I guarantee you that your prose will flow much more effectively. You will find it easier to articulate your answers, and in turn, your lecturers and markers will be increasingly able to locate and examine the core arguments and principals within your work.

If you struggle with writing essays and other forms of academic writing, think of yourself as a screenwriter. You are composing a script for your next Hollywood blockbuster on the subject of *your topic* Your characters are your arguments, and how they interact with each other are the voices of those who might support or disagree with your theories. Alternatively, you can think of yourself as a lawyer, building your concrete wall of evidence brick by brick and delivering it in a factual, concise and even sometimes dramatic way!

As with every new academic method, it doesn't work for everyone — but it's worth being mindful of this as an option. I have recommended this to many a student, and I have watched their writing transform in weeks, not months. You could transform your writing too…and it's as simple as being yourself and allowing your personality and understanding of the topic to do the work for you.

THINGS ARE GOING WRONG!
"THIS DEGREE IS POINTLESS AND I'VE HAD ENOUGH"

My first thing to say on this topic is: I FEEL YOUR PAIN! We've all had this thought cross our minds. Even the most high-flying professors who are at top of their field and leading the way for the progression of the industry have had doubts. We've all wanted to throw the towel in and blow our savings on travelling around Australia. I absolutely, totally, know where you're coming from. In actual fact, being in the midst of my PhD studies at the moment, I've had to remind myself very recently that it is all only temporary.

From my experience, it will start with a little tingle of frustration. It might not necessarily have made it to full blown doubt at this point, but you might start to find parts of your usual routine tedious and unfulfilling. Having lived through the stages of full-blown doubt and utter lack of enthusiasm to continue studying, take it from me that it's best to treat this initial frustration as a warning sign. When you're only mildly disillusioned, just a few small adjustments can have you back in a good headspace and ready and raring to continue. You could try any of the following steps, in any particular order to try and help get things back on track — and quickly:

Change an area of your weekly routine.
This can be as simple as shopping in Morrison's as opposed to Tesco, or moving your dedicated study hours to a different time of day or day of the week. If you're already studying on a Friday afternoon, perhaps you might work

more effectively if you tried placing your study on a Tuesday morning (if this works within your timetable of course) Alternatively, you can build in time for a new activity. Maybe you could build in a couple of hours to dedicate yourself to some time at the gym or reading?

Book a tutorial and be honest and open with your personal tutor/module tutor

While module tutors will be able to provide you with complete and comprehensive information relating to the particular class that they teach, you will most likely also have what we call a "personal tutor" This is the case for most institutions. A personal tutor is a member of staff (who may or may not teach any of the modules that you study) responsible for the care and welfare of a particular year group. This is the staff member you would go to with any concerns of a more general nature, and this is also the person who can help in putting any individual support plans in place. During my bachelor's degree, I was a little (more like A LOT) scared of my personal tutor, and I was probably more likely to win an Olympic gold medal for rhythmic gymnastics (I can't even cartwheel) than I was to sit down with them and talk about my worries. However, my master's degree was a different story. If you have an approachable member of staff who also happens to be your personal tutor, it is well worth a sit down with them to talk honestly and openly about your feelings. Sometimes, when things really aren't going your way, there can be more drastic options open to you (such as changing modules, or study groups) that can all be explored in a face to face meeting — but you won't know what any of these options are unless you put your cards on the table and open the dialogue. While some lecturers and personal tutors will actively enquire as to whether anyone needs any support, regrettably, not all are as approachable, and some are just so busy that it hasn't crossed their mind. That's not to say that they won't be able to help — but you must set the wheels in motion.

Alternatively, if there is a member of staff you get on particularly well with, you would always be able and welcome to book a tutorial with them. Sometimes they may refer you back to your personal tutor, but in some cases, they can take this role on for you...if you ask them nicely!

<u>Refer back to that "goal list" and remind yourself why you're there!</u>
This is something I say A LOT to my students. University is something of a black hole time loop. Once you're drawn in, the tendency is to completely forget the world outside. (Maybe that's why, even though I'm now working professionally, I still can't stop studying!)

I think this is part of the reason why so many people struggle with the enormity of the transition between university student and professional worker. In actual fact, the transition shouldn't really be that big — university is training you to do a job, which you then go out and do.
But of course, it's all too easy to fall into the trap of "eternal student-hood" (Some of us never stop!)

So, with this in mind, it always good to try to remain mindful of the reasons you enrolled on a university degree course in the first place. What is that dream job that inspired you enough to invest three years and a lot of money into an intense and direct training programme for that particular profession?

In my experience, it's always at around eight weeks in to the winter semester that people start to feel a bit down about this. I always try to have a "pick-me-up" happy class around this time, that recaps on what we've covered and checks in with our long-term goals. If you feel this would be beneficial to you, it's worth chatting with your module tutor about it — I'm sure they would be happy and willing to build it in to the course content!

In the meantime, keep writing down those lists that give voice to your long-term ambitions as well as those annoying little daily admin tasks. They may just help dig you out of a motivational hole later on!

<u>See what wellbeing services are on offer at your institution</u>
Every university (and of course its members of staff) has a duty of care to safeguard its students; academically, physically and of course mentally and emotionally. The education system and its awareness and implementation of various support networks has come a long way, even from when I was studying for my bachelor's degree just five years ago! Either the student services team or the student union will be best placed to point you in the direction of the wellbeing support available to you. You could be offered some counselling to talk through your thoughts and worries — or you could be navigated to a student-run wellbeing group that might have study group meetings, academic support sessions and perhaps even yoga classes!

It's always better to ask for help — and it doesn't mean

you've been any less successful in your university endeavours. If anything, it means that you've got more life experience!

Apply for mitigation (if appropriate)

Lecturers (and universities as a whole) realise that sometimes circumstances arise that are beyond your control, which may mean that you find yourself unable to complete an assignment or an exam at the right time. Mitigation exists so that students who find themselves in positions such as these are given some extra time to ease the pressure of deadlines and complete the assignment to the best of their ability. The process of applying for mitigation can vary between universities, so make sure that you're aware of how your particular institution handles these applications. There is usually a time criteria, to any mitigation application. You are usually able to apply any time before your exam, but there is commonly an ability to submit your application no later than seven days after your particular deadline. Sometimes you don't realise the effect that your circumstances have had on you until you actually have to sit the exam, or complete an assessment. Nevertheless, be sure to check what your university's time plan is, and avoid submitting too late!

Sometimes mitigation applications can be made online via your particular student portal, but other times they can be made direct to your module tutor, module leader or course leader. Alternatively, you can seek the guidance of your personal tutor, who may be able to action this process on your behalf. Depending on your particular mitigating circumstances, you may be required to provide evidence to back up your application. This will usually be in the form of a doctor's note or other official document that verifies your circumstances. Of course, such documents and personal notes will be handled with the strictest confidence.

There is absolutely no shame in applying for mitigation. A lot of students have got in touch with me with concerns that applying for/receiving mitigation will have a negative impact on their final degree classification or module grade — but this is not the case at all. In the same way that any employer may grant compassionate leave when personal circumstances mean that someone isn't able to attend work, mitigation exists as a support network that allows you to complete your assignments in exactly the same way — just with an extra time allowance. It has no impact on your marks or ability to progress further with your studies. If you think mitigation will help ease any worry or anxiety, talk it through with your module/personal tutor, and they will help you to action the process.

As I touched on above, there are sometimes more drastic options available if you're really not happy with your current situation — and in the spirit of being completely and totally honest with you, I myself needed to use some of these measures during my bachelor's degree.

The first of these is changing your module selection. While most universities will have uniform modules for everyone in their first year of study, it's often the case that you are given "options" for your second year and beyond. This allows you to choose a "specialism" and follow a study path more appropriate for your particular desired line of work. Sometimes, choosing to change your option selection will be possible (if you're not already too far into the module workload) This can help rid you of any modules that you're just not enjoying, and could potentially offer you enough of a change to your existing routine to allow you to settle back down into the swing of things. This comes with a disclaimer though: Do not use this as an "outer" for a module that's just too hard!

If you're struggling academically, please use the various support options available before you make any drastic decisions. Some modules are compulsory, but for the ones that are option-selected, you chose the ones you did because they appealed to you more than the rest!

Let knowing that circumstances are always able to change give you peace of mind, but don't let this allow you to lose any of your academic ambition. Your staff are there to support you in becoming the best professional you can be...use them — and don't jump to a compromise because one module is a bit harder than the alternatives.

The other options, and these are more drastic, are changing course — and sometimes even transferring university completely. Now, I'll hold my hands up and tell you that I changed course in my first week of study, not once — but twice! In all honestly, I found the course I was accepted on just too daunting! Not even academically — but socially! The general intake was absolutely massive, everyone seemed like confident extroverts, and I just knew that I wasn't going to fit in. Therefore, rather than spending my first weeks of university toiling away and getting permanently put off by the whole thing, I decided to swap courses. I then swapped again! (The second swap was switching around the subject I was 'majoring' in and 'minoring" in) Eventually I found the combination that worked, and was much happier for it. If you want to swap around within your institution, you should speak to your course leader who will be able to liaise with other course leaders on your behalf. If, however, you've fallen out of love with the university as a whole (and this does happen!) you can talk to the admissions offices of other institutions that take your fancy to discuss your options. Once you have a clear idea of the route you want to take and the requirements of this transfer, you will be able to talk to your academic administration office (generally with a specific officer for your course) to facilitate whatever needs to be arranged.

The fact of the matter is; things do go wrong. Life would be very boring if everything went right all the time! My biggest advice to you is; don't make these decisions alone. Always give voice to your doubts and thought processes, because you may find that things are able to be resolved much more rapidly. Don't make any rushed decisions, and always make use of the support networks available.

LOOKING AFTER YOUR MENTAL HEALTH

No matter what challenges get thrown at you during your time at university, looking after yourself is the most important one. Sometimes, self-care can indeed feel like a challenge - particularly In a fast-paced, mentally demanding and socially active environment like university. BUT THIS MUST ALWAYS BE YOUR TOP PRIORITY. After all, the key ingredient in your recipe for success is...yourself — and as such, you must try to keep yourself in the best physical and mental position possible. Sometimes though, this can fall by the wayside — and the last thing you need me to do is preach at you on the importance of getting your self-care routine back on track.

Over the course of your studies, it's not uncommon to have a dip in your mental health, you may experience:

- Stress (which can be exacerbated by exams and deadlines)
- Anxiety (both academically, personally and socially)
- Low self-esteem (academically and personally, low self-esteem can be persistent and can relate to many different areas)
- Pressure (this can be triggered by your own expectations of yourself, or by people around you)
- Imposter syndrome (the sense of doubt in your own achievements and the feeling that you are something of a fraud and don't belong in your particular position)

Of course, these are just a few of the more common issues you might experience — and if you are feeling any one or more of these things, the last thing you're going to want/need to hear from me is a load of pleas to look after yourself. Instead, I'll let you know that I have struggled and continue to struggle with all of the above. Therefore, instead of preaching, I'll share with you some of the things I found, and continue to find most useful both as a doctoral student and a member of university staff. Before I do though, a little disclaimer: you should always talk to a professional if you need advice or guidance on dealing with your mental health. There are many books, and of course qualified professionals out there to explain how to improve and safeguard your mental health far better than I can — these are just some of my insights on how I dealt with my own mental health from the position that you're in now or might find yourself in at some time or other during your studies.

Initial things to try yourself:

Limit your use of social media — I know this may be tricky, but looking at other people's lives inevitably leads you to compare them to your own. The fact of the matter is, you can't believe anything you see on social media! Limit your use and you will feel more
content, and more able to focus.

Make a "brain dump" — For me, this is one of the best kind of lists. The basic principal of this is, write down EVERYTHING in your mind. Even if it's as mundane as "I need to do the washing" or as big as "I'm worried I'm not going to pass my degree", get it all out. Here you can also write things that you wouldn't necessarily say aloud (and in the spirit of honestly, I'll share one of my brain dump entries with you) Write down things like *"I'm worrying about what other people achieve instead of concerning myself with my own marks. I'm putting so many hours in, but other people who don't seem to be studying as much are achieving higher marks. Is this because my tutor doesn't like me?"*

Writing a physical note like this will help you rid your mind of all those nagging, persistent thoughts so you can think more clearly. From making those nagging thoughts visual, you can start to apply logic and sort through it. In the above example, it's clear that at least some of this is my own paranoia, but some of it may be resolved by speaking to either the student union or the lecturer in question. That then becomes something to add to my "to-do" list! Most of the time, writing down negative thoughts was enough for me to dispel any anger I had. Have you ever penned a REALLY ANGRY response to an annoying email to make you feel better, and then not sent it? (My hand's in the air ten times over!) This is essentially the same thing. You can then use your brain dump to inform any "to do lists" you've got on the go. Once everything's out in the open and in one place, you'll start to feel a bit better.

Make a "control chart" – For me, this would usually come after writing out my brain dump (though it works just fine if you just do this part on its own!) Looking through the notes of everything going on inside my head, I would often find that a good 80% of my worries were about things that I simply had no control or influence over. I would be worried about scenarios that may or may not happen, or whether an exam was going to fall on a certain day which would clash with an existing arrangement – but the fact of the matter is, I couldn't control any of this.

Using the examples above, I can't control what *Emma* gets graded for a particular assignment, nor is it important to my own development. However, I CAN control whether I do the washing or not, or whether I do enough work to pass a certain module. I can't control the dates of assessments or whether my final exam clashes with my friend's birthday party, but I CAN control preparing everything in advance so that if a clash does happen, I can be prepared enough to ace the exam and then ready to head out straight away afterwards. Sometimes I liked to split a piece of paper into two columns: things I can control and things to let go of, and then take everything on my brain dump and sort it out. Other times, I'd just make a list of "action points" i.e. things I can actually do something about, whilst eliminating and forgetting about everything else.

In either case, my thoughts were much clearer and I found that with a more organised mind, I could get more done and retain more information – thus improving my levels of stress and my mental health.

Go for regular walks/exercise – You've probably heard this one lots, but it really does work. Fresh air and a bit of endorphins can do wonders if you're looking to rid yourself of a bit of stress and anxiety.

Limit your caffeine (says the coffee addict!) – It's a case of "do as I say and not as I do with this one!" I know just how tempting it is to rely on Americanos to see you through the day, but I sometimes find that this can cause lots of midday energy crashes and can actually disrupt sleep – which is vital for maintaining good physical and mental health. If you are a coffee addict (like me), see if you can cut down just a little bit. You might notice some substantial changes in the way you feel!

Try some "flow state" activities – I remember going to a really interesting seminar in my third year of study relating to the "flow state" and what it can do for you.

Essentially, the "flow state" is when you're doing an activity and not consciously thinking about a) carrying out the particular activity at that moment, or b) anything else that could distract your mind. You know, when you're in the middle of a PlayStation game or something, and you're totally immersed in that activity while not being consciously aware of what you're doing – that's flow state. When you actually put a name to it and identify it as a state of mind that can be achieved, you think to yourself "oh yeah, it's great when that happens. All of my worries just go away" – and when you're actively in flow state, this is true. The key elements of flow state are focus, energy and enjoyment – it's not flow state if you're not enjoying yourself – by the nature that you're finding the activity boring or tedious, you are distracted! What you'll be pleased to hear is that it's not just counterproductive activities that allow you to get "in flow", you can achieve flow state when writing an essay, or during an exam – when you're totally and completely in the zone, you're there! When working on anything academic or study-related, achieving "flow" increases your productivity, which reduces stress and ultimately boosts your morale. However, it can be just as beneficial to your mental health to build some time into your day to carry out a "mindless activity." You should never feel guilty about putting aside some time to play a game, read a book or listen to music and be totally absorbed in it. This has great power in reducing your stress and anxiety levels, allowing you to feel calmer and more in control – which in turn, will improve your academic work!

Try some yoga/mediation – Now, I'll be honest with you – yoga and meditation is something I've always wanted to get into, but I've never found the time to properly throw myself into it. I've done little bits here and there, but not enough to become properly hooked on it. Having said this, I am CONSTANTLY hearing good things about the power of yoga and meditation and their ability to improve your focus and mental health. Before committing to paying for set classes, try some free tutorials at home to see if it's something that could work for you. Like everything, it won't work for everyone, but you might just find it a lifesaver!

Then of course you have the options to talk to your university support teams (usually based inside the student services team) who will be able to:

- Point you in the direction of professionals (counselling/further support)
- Set up regular wellbeing meetings with a member of staff
- Talk to staff on your behalf
- Set up an individual support plan which is circulated to your lecturers highlighting any specific needs
- Point you in the direction of any internal university support groups that can provide ongoing help

One thing I will say though is: No matter how hard you work or how high or low your grades are, mental health problems can affect anyone. People at the very top of their profession struggle with stress and self-doubt, and with the every-changing and unique environment that university is, it's not out of the ordinary to find yourself struggling. The best thing to do is not to let the problem get out of hand. Address it, talk to people and make use of the support networks available. There's not an exam in the world that is more important than your own health and wellbeing.

Remember that if you are in a good mental headspace, you are far more likely to be able to achieve and realise your potential — so don't suffer in silence, and do allow yourself to be supported — there really is no shame in accepting help.

WAYS TO EXCEL: HOW TO MAKE YOUR MARK AND GO THE EXTRA MILE

Just like the world of work, university can get competitive. Whilst this can be stressful and can cause a bit of anxiety and tension amongst friends and study groups – it can actually be quite a good thing. Competition exists in all areas of life – it's the reason we have evolved into the humans we are today! Every job interview and audition is a competition – and every essay you submit and exam you sit is essentially a competition with yourself. Once you get used to how competition finds its way into each part of your personal and university life, you can make peace with it – and it can actually help to spur you on and achieve even greater things!

Obviously the most successful way to make a good impression with your lecturers and get the best out of your degree is to maintain consistently high grades. However, this may not always be realistic, or indeed feel like the most interesting of endeavours. In this case, there are other ways to make a good impression and go the extra mile – all while supporting the continued success of your studies:

Become a course rep
Every course will have a representative that attends occasional planning meetings with members of staff. They will be able to collate the general views and concerns of the course cohort and present these to the appropriate lecturers and support staff so that any adjustments can be made. This is generally a voluntary position, but one that allows you to

communicate directly with senior staff, and it looks very good on your CV going forwards. You will be expected to open lines of communication between students and staff, engage with your fellow students to gather opinions and suggestions and report these back when requested.

Take on a role within the student union
Inevitably, as students are always graduating and moving on, there are always roles for the taking within the student union — and some of them can pay too!

These can be administrative and in more of an "office setup" but they can also involve going out and surveying students to find out what more can be done by the union to improve the service that they offer. There is "National Student Union Awards" every year — and everyone wants the top spot!

If you're looking to enter an industry that relies heavily on good communication, engagement with others and leadership, a role within the student union would look FANTASTIC on your CV. Not only does it show that you are competent and up to the job, but it also demonstrates that you are passionate about improving the experiences of others — and this is the backbone and core ethos of several industries and companies. Perhaps more selfishly, it can also provide you with a closer link to senior union staff, which may mean that you'll have an easier time of accessing help, should you ever need to.

Start a student society
As I touched on previously, your student union will offer a wide range of activities and opportunities for engagement outside of your course requirements. Whilst a lot of these will be union-run activities, there will be an array of student

societies which can diversify the range of activities on offer even further.

If, however, you identify a "gap in the market", you might like to consider starting your own! It looks fantastic on your CV and is also a way of securing a lasting legacy at the university for many years to come!

Most societies have to be given the green light by the student union, and there will be a few hoops that you may have to jump through:

- Have a meeting with a student union officer to
- discuss your idea to see if it is an appropriate fit
- Recruit a chairman, secretary, treasurer and membership secretary
- Hold a meeting to discuss how the society will be funded (usually through the payment of subscription fees)
- Clarify what students get for their membership
- Present this to your student union officer
- Then start to run your society!
- You will be required to check in with your student union officer as you meet certain milestones – but they will be able to discuss this in more detail with you, as the process may be different for your particular institution.

Of course, if starting a student society from scratch is not something that appeals to you, there is always the option of taking on one of the official positions (chairman, secretary, treasurer etc.) within an existing society. You will still get the benefit of an enhanced CV, as well as all of the social benefits that come with being involved in a student-run society.

Become a student ambassador

Remember when I spoke about enrolment and being almost blinded by a sea of students in t-shirts so yellow that they were almost a light source? – well those lovely students were "student ambassadors"

An ambassador role can come in many different guises, and here are just some of the things you might be required to do if you take on such a role:

Be present at open days and be willing to talk to prospective students/give tours etc.

Take on public relations roles at other university events. This could mean mixing with sponsors and donors at showcases or facilitating with front-of-house at performances or exhibitions.

Work within the library or student services teams to guide and assist newer students.

Occasionally set up rooms ahead of lectures and be responsible for collecting any equipment that is needed for that particular session.

Mentor

Put simply, it is a position of trust that will see you acting as a student representative of your university and will often require you to mix with members of the public (from prospective students to senior members of the governing body!)

To be an effective student ambassador, you will need

excellent communication skills, confidence, leadership qualities — but these can be learnt on the job! There's no need to be a professional sales person or motivational speaker from the get-go — if you have a friendly face, are passionate about your studies and are happy to share this with others, you would be an excellent ambassador!

Again, this looks wonderful on your CV, but also helps you to get out and about. You may meet students who you will end up working with both within and outside of university, but you could also meet sponsors, donors and employers who may be interested in supporting you in pursing your chosen career!

It's well worth considering!

<u>Apply for any funding and scholarships available to further your research</u>
This is kind of an extension of what I've said above: Many universities have sponsors and donors who have established funds within the institution. For example, some individuals (let's say John and Betty Smith) give the university £500 a year under the umbrella of "The John and Betty Smith Bursary" This bursary is then able to be applied for once a year. Sometimes there are stipulations (like the student must be studying for a degree relating to the hospitality industry) and sometimes there aren't. Sometimes, there are competitions to determine the winner of said monies.
It's worth checking out what's available.
Any extra funding helps further your research capabilities, which will in turn improve both your overall classification and your CV going forwards!

Volunteer for any appropriate student showcases/open days/events

This one kind of goes without saying. Of course, taking any and all opportunities to show off your work will make a good impression and raise your profile, both as a student and as a new professional entering the industry.

You know what they say, "any publicity is good publicity", but it's lovely to showcase your work for the first time within the safe and confidence-building university environment, so that you're better prepared for any presentations you have to make in the professional industry!

STUDENT SURVEYS EXPLAINED
WHY YOUR LECTURERS KEEP BADGERING YOU TO
COMPLETE THEM, AND HOW THEY CAN HELP YOU

As a lecturer, I know that I drive my students ABSOLUTELY
POTTY when the time for the surveys comes around.
Members of staff are always encouraged by senior
members of the faculty to badger students to submit their
responses — some will even allow them to be completed in
class time.

What's become apparent from being a source of annoyance
for many of my students is that the vast majority find surveys
irrelevant and are not entirely sure of what they mean and
how they can impact them.

Let me explain just a few of the most common ones to you, so
you know why they're important:

MODULE EVALUATION SURVEY (MES)

This gives you the opportunity to give feedback about the
content and quality of teaching for each module you study.
The responses to this survey are likely to have the strongest
ability to make substantial changes, both immediately and
long term. Unlike lots of other surveys, which aim to set long-
term goals, the module evaluation survey is uniquely placed
to facilitate direct changes and improvements that can be
implemented almost straight away. This is the survey I stress
the most to my students for this very reason. As a lecturer, if
the module is not meeting your needs — I want to know about
it, so it can be rectified! On the flip side; if you absolutely
love the module, then it's a welcome pick-me-up and
reassurance that I'm meeting all of your needs and

expectations. We're always grateful for responses and guidance, so please do play your part!

NATIONAL STUDENT SURVEY (NSS)

This is an annual, nationalised survey that all final year undergraduates are invited to complete. You will be asked a core group of questions relating to your university experience as follows:

- The overall quality of teaching
- Opportunities for learning
- Assessments and feedback
- Academic support available
- Overall organisation and management
- Learning resources available
- Learning community
- Student voice
- Your overall satisfaction with your institution

Responses to the NSS are collated by an independent party, and universities use the information from responses provided to make real and lasting changes in line with the needs and requirements of its students. <u>Your university should not influence your responses in any way.</u>

There are some achievements available if a university performs particularly well in a certain area of the survey (such as teaching awards if the overall teaching quality has a high level of satisfaction) and this in turn can determine fee structures and number university places available — so your responses really do matter. If you're a final year student, think back to when you were a timid first-year — I'm sure you'd be grateful for final year students giving open and honest responses to make things better for you during your time at the university. This is not just your chance to make lasting change, but also to give back.

STUDENT UNION SURVEYS

Student Union Surveys aren't nationalised and can vary dramatically between institutions. Some universities won't issue surveys directly, and instead will recruit student "engagement officers" who will be paid to talk to students on campus and gather general opinions, or phone you directly to ask for responses (this is a particularly common role for new alumni — i.e. those who have left the university recently.)

There are some cases where your student union may put together an online survey which will be circulated to all students. This is usually to determine your overall satisfaction level relating to the service the union is providing, which extends to the variety of activities on offer, quality of academic support and the access to facilities to name a few! (Sometimes, there may be a prize incentive to taking part — so it's worth getting involved!)

Be mindful when completing these particular surveys that it is not very common that you will have experienced the FULL range of student union services — so to protect the integrity of the overall responses, make sure you only answer the parts that relate to you!

THE END OF SECOND YEAR: THE SECOND (AND LAST) SUMMER HOLIDAY

If you're studying for a three-year degree, the second time you break up for an official summer holiday will be your last. (If you're studying a four-year course, let's just apply this to your third summer break!) This can be a very daunting thought. Think back to last summer when you suddenly realised you had all this spare time at your disposal. Your studies were abandoned for four blissful months as you relished not having to stress about the pressure of final exams or assessments that would be on the horizon the minute you returned to study. Suddenly, just eight months down the line, you find yourself in the same situation — but this time with the dawning realisation that, barring any further full-time degree, this would be your last opportunity to be "busy doing nothing" before final exams, graduation and the world of work beckoned! Being a bit of a worrier myself, this is something I did struggle with when I broke up for the summer break at the end of my second year. I had this persistent inner monologue that went something like: "Enjoy yourself this summer, because this is probably the last chance you're going to get to properly enjoy yourself for a while…but don't waste the whole summer because otherwise you'll already be behind when you start back in September – and you don't want to finish uni and be stuck with nothing prepared" – Do you agree that I'm a worrier yet?!

If your mind is similar to mine, (and even if it isn't), I'm here to tell you as someone with experience: **Achievement and enjoyment go hand in hand!**

You need to enjoy your summer – of course you do…and when you feel happier in yourself for having let your hair down a bit, you'll achieve far more when you next sit down and focus.

The same goes for the other way around: If you work hard and dedicate some (not lots) of time to getting things prepared, both for your academic year and beyond (I'll go into this in a minute), then you'll enjoy yourself more when you stop the work to do something fun. Without the background worry, you'll feel much better!

As I mentioned before, this summer period is a fantastic opportunity to get the ball rolling on preparing for your entry into the industry as a fully-fledged professional! Just in case you need a bit of inspiration, here are a few things you can do to get yourself in the best possible position:

Preparing for your final year of university:

Make any "option" decisions early

There are some cases (particularly for final year modules) where you will be invited to select your chosen modules for the following academic year. This allows you to choose your own study path and refine or indeed broaden your knowledge, should you wish to specialise in a particular area to focus your learning. From my experience of both sides of the lectern, the biggest early stress of the final university year is not making this decision early enough. Believe it or not, some students arrive back for the start of their final year without having chosen their options. If they still don't choose in time, they are often allocated a choice generally based on the module with the least take up, so the teaching numbers can be equalised. Please don't let this happen to you! Granted, you are sometimes able to change modules if you've realised early enough through the process that you're not happy with your choice, but this is not always the case. Don't leave this decision hanging over you for the whole of the summer holiday either.

Make your choice early, so you can both secure your place on the module and prepare the relevant work for it.

Get your study materials in place at the start of the holiday
This is another piece of advice that probably goes without saying, but there's something almost therapeutic about packing a bag ahead of when you actually need to use it.

Ask any mother preparing her hospital bag for birth! (It's always best to be prepared!)

Throwing things into a rucksack last minute is always going to increase your chances of forgetting something, and it'll put you in a far greater headspace and position for success if you start your last year of study as you mean to go on. This also means ordering or getting together any specific study materials you need so you have them in good time. Are you going to need to buy or borrow any books from relevant reading lists? Perhaps you need a certain type of paper and pen, music or piece of equipment? If so, get it now so you don't have to worry about it later!

Sort out your finances

Money is always such a dreadful thing to be worrying about. By now, I'm sure you'll have all of your student finance loan/maintenance loan/other funding source all sorted and settled – however, it's always useful to budget how any living costs will be spent, particularly for your last year where expenses in portfolio resources, study materials or simply nights out to celebrate how far you've come are likely to be higher. If you're stressing and worrying about your financial situation, you'll find yourself less able to focus on achieving your best academically – and that's a no win situation! I know it's not easy for everybody, but there is always help available, and any university student services team usually operates over the summer period and will be able to give you advice and guidance as and when you might need it.

Start planning your final portfolio

Whatever you're studying, there is a very strong chance that one of your final assignments will be some kind of portfolio presentation to showcase your work and indeed your specialism. From the moment that I saw final year students present their final showcases as a quiet and timid first-year student, I started to plan and brainstorm ideas for my own. Granted, they only ever stayed in the back of my mind – that is until I realised that my whole university experience had gone by in the blink of an eye, and I found myself actively rushing to get the bloody thing done! Make sure you note down whatever ideas you have as and when you have them – who knows, you might just come up with something remarkable! If you're absolutely certain of what the assignment criteria is at your university (perhaps it's always the same for all final year students), and you're equally certain of what you want to present, there's no reason why you can't start prepping before your studies actually kick in! Use the time when there's no other academic pressure or background stress to get the ball rolling. With a clear mind, you'll have an easier time of focussing your efforts, and you'll find that you're able to get well ahead if you want to. I've worked with many a panicked student who left their final showcase plans to the very last minute, and in every case, they have achieved a lower grade than they could have got (across the board, not just in this one assignment.) I'm really not trying to scare you or put you off – in fact, the opposite! If you spread the workload and work little and often over the course of the summer break, you'll have much more time to get things right academically – and in turn, much more time to have much more fun!

Preparing for the beyond:

<u>Think ahead to putting together your professional package</u>
I'll go into a bit more detail about this later, but your final summer holiday in between academic years is the perfect opportunity to start laying your professional foundations so you can hit the ground running just as soon as you graduate. Start to put your CV together and scan for opportunities to see what roles are being advertised that suit your skills. If you're struggling to decide which academic options to take for your final year, perhaps scouting opportunities might help you choose. Are there more positions available for those who are expert in a particular field, for instance? Of course, any industry is always adapting and evolving to suit

the changing needs of the modern consumer, but seeing what roles are out there can be a very good indicator if you need a little bit of inspiration.

Diversify your final year's study accordingly

Having looked at the various job options available in your chosen field, you would have had a chance to familiarise yourself with what key skills employers are looking for. Do all the job specifications state that experience in public speaking is a must? If so, why not join a debate or presentation-based society during your final year? If problem solving is a key skill, then you could look to find work within the student union, assisting with academic appeals or the resolution of complaints.

Make the most of student subscriptions and join appropriate societies

Are the any societies, unions or organisations that are particularly prevalent in your industry? Will having a professional membership to such organisations improve your employability and provide you with useful assistance in finding a job after you've graduated? Could your membership of a particular professional society also be something else to speak about at a potential job interview? If so, you might like to think about joining one now! Some of these organisations have the option to subscribe for three year's membership upfront, and if this is at a discounted student fee, then you simply can't let that opportunity pass you by! You might want to hold off until your graduation is a little closer in order to maximise length of membership when you first enter the workplace, but I have found that students have found it very handy to have the advice, tips, opportunities and literature that comes with membership over the duration of their final year's study. This has helped them refine their learning in line with the changes within the industry and has helped them become all the more aware of what the workplace will be like, and how they can fit into it most effectively.

Can you look for any appropriate work experience that will enhance both your studies and your overall employability?

With time on your hands over the course of the summer holiday, why not try to secure some work experience in your particular chosen profession? This will not only prove a valuable addition to your CV (which will make you a more attractive candidate to recruiters), but could also be used as part of your studies. For instance, you may well be taking a module in your final year that calls for some kind of work placement. If this is the case, then perhaps this experience would suffice? Alternatively, one of your assignments may be a written report or essay on something to do with your chosen profession. If so, perhaps you could use your work experience to greater inform your written work, providing real-world examples to support any academic or theoretical findings. This would show a great sense of initiative and innovation to your lecturer and will be sure to earn you a better mark overall.

It may well be the case that, over the course of your final year, your tuition focuses on professional and industry practice more thoroughly. That's fantastic if it is the case, but it doesn't always happen. The fact of the matter is, whether you're offered "industry training" as part of your degree or not, there is no one better to determine how you as an individual will fit into the workplace than yourself. Once you're fully aware of what your ambitions are and the steps that you have to take in order to achieve them, nothing will stand in your way but your own motivation. However, if you're inspired and raring to succeed, then even this won't stop you!

Make sure you have fun this summer. If I'm brutally honest with you, it may well be the longest period of time you have "off" in a good while...but use it wisely. Make the most of all the moments to build the foundations, as well as relaxing your mental and physical health, so you put yourself in the best possible position for success when studies recommence in September.

LOOKING AHEAD: THE HOME STRETCH!

By your third year of study, you'll undoubtedly be thinking ahead to your future careers and how you can make big strides towards achieving your ultimate ambitions – and so you should be! Going to university is that vital stepping stone between early adulthood and becoming a fully-functioning professional. You've not just honed the academics of your craft, but you've also perfected the art of self-discipline, independence, managing your time and work ethic, multi-tasking, working to deadlines and performing under pressure. This is on top of social networking, communication and keeping calm in a crisis – (all of those slightly fraught pub visits would have taught you something!) You are almost ready to enter the world of work. You are almost ready to make your mark on your chosen industry – and your contribution, however big or small, will help the capabilities of your profession to grow and expand.

It was towards the end of the first semester of my final year that I really started to think about what on earth I was going to do afterwards. I was daunted by the prospect of leaving the institution that had become so much a part of my routine that I saw it as something of a safety net…in short, I didn't want to go. BUT any and every university will not simply dump you on a
roadside with a suitcase, a degree and a dog-eared bus ticket to your first ever interview.

As you are probably aware, each university is independently "assessed" on a number of criteria to determine its place on various league tables. It's these league tables that rank how good a university is and in turn, makes places to study there more desirable. One of the areas that each university is "assessed" on, is what percentage of their students are in employment within 6 months/a year of graduating.

Now, this is a fairly ambiguous statistic, and if I had my way I would rephrase that question to ask what percentage of their students are in employment IN THEIR CHOSEN INDUSTRY within 6 months/a year of graduating to greater determine the success of specialised courses. Nevertheless, I'll try not to get too wound up about it!

In my case, I actually got my first job in the industry through the university channel. To make this clearer, I didn't receive a direct recommendation from the university, but the job I went on to get was circulated to university students as a result of the institution's link with the job advertiser. This was a fantastic job that I would NEVER have found out about had it not pinged through in an email to my university account! It's always worth remembering that a lot of universities have partnerships of various kinds with some of the most high-profile businesses spanning a variety of industries. As a result of these partnerships, businesses sometimes offer universities the opportunity for students to apply for roles either exclusively or ahead of other applicants.

Having said this, whether applying for a job through the university's existing links or not, there will be a diverse range of support available to you (and I will go into more detail later when I talk about your "professional package") Just some of the support available may include:

- CV workshops

- Mock interviews/classes on interview technique
- Free or reduced rate subscriptions to appropriate professional bodies
- Jobs fair organised by the university

This is a BIG ONE. Usually in the summer term when people are thinking about where they are moving on to, the university may organise a jobs fair on campus. Companies who are looking to hire new staff members, or organisations partnered with the university with opportunities will come along and host a stall where you are able to find out more/apply for jobs! Think of it like the "ideal home show" but with companies directly looking for people like you to join them!

It's SO worth finding out if/when something like this is happening and putting the date firmly in your diary. Whilst nothing may come of it, it's a chance to mix with people actively working in your chosen industry, and may give you more job options later on!

The biggest thing I have watched students fall down on is not putting an action plan in place before leaving the university. Just think about it, whilst you may still be able to get "alumni perks" once you've left your place of study, it's never easier to get support than when you're a student! All the appropriate teams are in place and ready for you to use — so of course the best thing to do is to make the most of them while you can!

When thinking ahead to the role you will play within your chosen industry, my biggest nugget of wisdom that underpins everything I say in the rest of this chapter is:

<u>FIND YOUR USP!</u>

USP = Unique Selling Point.

This is usually applied to products or brands – but sometimes it helps to think of *yourself* as a brand! Put simply, your unique selling point is; what makes you different to everyone else? What can you do that others can't do, or can't do as effectively and efficiently? Do you have a unique skill set that would make waves in a particular industry? Do you have a unique combination of skills that make you one of a kind? In the same way that you'd sell a car or a washing machine, what is it about you that makes you better than every other option?

Now, this is particular prevalent in the performing arts and music industries where a role in a film might require somebody who can sing, but is also an expert in karate – a VERY strange combination, but believe me, it's been done! However, that's not to say that you can't identify your USP in any and all other areas. Do you have a specialist knowledge of a particular area in business management, but are also a skilled actor or public speaker? If so, you could "pitch" yourself as someone who is able to host and hold conferences and large-scale events, as well as the carrying out the day-to-day requirements of the role! Do you see what I'm getting at?

Whenever I talk to my students about identifying and building upon your USP, I'm sometimes met with blank faces. "But I don't know what mine is!" (I hear a lot) "Can you tell me what mine is, because I haven't got a clue?!"

The fact of the matter is, while your lecturers will be able to advise you on what they feel is your particular skill set, and any assignment or exam marks you have received may further help to point this out for you, you are best placed to identify what you feel are your strongest areas. For instance, I once spoke to a student who said, "everybody always says my confidence is my biggest strength, but I actually hate public speaking – I'm just good at pretending that I'm not nervous!" You'd be surprised at how often I've heard this! My reply is:

"Your USP has to be the best combination of your achievements and your personal boundaries. Regardless of whether you've achieved consistently top marks in speech assignments, there's no point selling yourself as an excellent motivational speaker if you want the ground to swallow you up every time you have to stand up in front of people. Your USP is your identifier of where you would be most effective within a company or the industry as a whole – where would you make the biggest difference? And remember that in order to make such a difference and be the most effective worker you can be, you have to always feel safe and comfortable!"

So, my advice to you is a good old spider diagram! (You know, those ones you learnt about in year 3 with the circle in the middle and loads of little legs drawn off of it?!)

Put your name in the circle in the middle and draw branches of that circle to identify your key strengths and skills (even if some of them seem random!). Once you've finished, try and combine them in a few words as possible – and there you have it. This can not only be your USP, but can also form the first line of any CV you might put together later down the line.

Let me show you:

If you come out with the following skills, and are looking to build a career as a lawyer for instance:

- Charity law specialism
- Good knowledge of Charity Commission procedure
- Good communication
- Good leadership skills
- Enjoy drawing and painting
- Very fast and efficient reader
- I could say my USP is:
- Combining knowledge with creativity and flair to make charity law more accessible for clients.

My opening line for my CV could then be something like:

I am a skilled and fully qualified lawyer with a specialist knowledge of charity law. I combine knowledge and skill with creativity and flair to make charity law more accessible for clients. This enables me to provide and consistently maintain an innovative and friendly professional service.

Now it's your turn to follow the process and fill in the blanks!

Understanding your USP will not only assist in your ability to network and promote yourself later on, but can also give you a massive boost of self-esteem at the point when it is most needed. It can help you to understand that you are in fact a very skilled individual on the brink of achieving great things. Let it be a reminder that the world is your oyster and opportunities are ripe, ready and yours for the taking!

THINKING ABOUT THAT FIRST JOB

My advice is to use the summer holiday before you return to your third (or final) year of study to start to explore what options are available to you. What vacancies are there currently and what will you require/need to put in place in order to apply? I've mentioned the importance of putting together your CV already, but you might like to consider what you can do during your final year to enhance your CV to suit the role you want to apply for? Are there any societies you can join or extra-circular activities that will enhance your skillset and support your academic development? You can then start to build your portfolio and train yourself for particular roles within your industry alongside your final year's study. As long as you are able to manage your time effectively and prioritise achieving the best possible results in your studies, there is no reason why you can't look ahead. It'll mean you're able to hit the ground running as soon as you graduate rather than having to start from nothing — which can of course be a very daunting prospect!

Thinking about your first job will be so exciting for you — but you may also find it the most terrifying thing you've ever done.

For the vast majority of people, your first job will be the first time you have ever ventured outside of full time education. This is the moment when all those times your parents said, "just wait until you're working" to you as a child, come to life. For me, it felt very liberating, but it also felt very permanent. A small part of me felt like I was "signing away my life", like I was committing myself to going "the full workaholic" with minimal annual leave, mortgages, conferences and wearing suits and pajamas in a constant demoralising rotation. In a way, I suppose it is like that: compared with school hours, university timetables are much more flexible and often involve a lot more remote working. This can be a little dangerous in giving you a false perception of what the workplace will actually be like. In many ways, I found the idea of sitting at a desk from 9-5pm much more like school (with the added bonus of unlimited coffee), and much less like university, which relies on your own initiative to get heavily involved in your learning. If you're worried about feeling this way (and believe me, I was), you have to try and reframe your mind-set: As I say to all of my students, working within the industry in whatever guise, is the true measure of your university success.

While your classification and exam results may get you through the door to an interview or may help you to land the job in the first instance, working within the industry on a daily basis means you have been successful in your university endeavours. Think back to why you wanted to attend university in the first place — to acquire the knowledge to enable you to work within your chosen industry in your chosen profession — and if you manage to work a job that allows you to do this...job well done!

If you think of it like this, succeeding doesn't seem so hard — in fact, it seems more than realistic...but INEVITABLE! The fact of the matter is, not everyone in the world is lucky enough to do a job that they love — and sometimes, a job you loved once can become tedious and boring a few years down the line. Don't be daunted by the word "permanent" because, in reality, nothing is. There are always ways to change, and there is always room to grow and adapt. Just use this time to establish your roots, focus your craft, and you will put yourself in the best possible place to make a profound and important impact on your industry. I guess everyone wants that perfect job, where they're totally and utterly content all day every day, but it's important to understand that sometimes it's better to get a foot in the door and progress within a company. We've all heard the stories of tea boy to CEO, studio runner to director- there is always a ladder to climb. Don't be disheartened by the possibility of having to start at the bottom — it just means that the only way is up!

FINAL EXAMS – HOW TO NAIL YOUR FINAL SUBMISSIONS!

Remember when I said earlier that your final year of university will go by in an absolute blur? Well, by the time you're thinking about taking your final exams, I'm sure you'll know exactly what I was talking about! Your induction day and enrolment will feel like they happened last week, and you'll suddenly realise that your family were dead right when they said, "it'll be over before you know it" all those hundreds of times! From navigating my way through the challenges of being an undergraduate student to setting and marking final exams as a lecturer, I know just how strange the final few months of university can be. I've seen bright and bubbly students suddenly become quite quiet and withdrawn, but I have also seen students lacking in confidence come out of their shell in an almost unrecognisable manner. The fact of the matter is, university is a mixing pot of challenges, emotions and experiences at the best of times – and throwing in the pressure of exams that will have a big impact on your final degree classification makes the process seem all the more daunting. Earlier on in this book I've talked about ways in which you can prepare yourself for assessments, improve your mental health and seek advice from internal university-run support groups – and in the case of preparing for your final exams, all of these tips still apply. Therefore, what I thought might be more useful is if I share with you some of the things that I often notice people forget to include (both for written exams and presentation based exams). Hopefully reading through these tips might trigger a lightbulb moment to include something that you might have forgotten about!

FOR WRITTEN EXAMS (ESSAYS/REPORTS/TESTS)

<u>References</u> – This is the biggest thing that people miss out. I'm always surprised by the number of students that forget to add references into their work. Backing up any conclusions that you've made with credible sources is VITAL. Sometimes, I've seen students use a quotation but forget to cite and reference it properly – sadly, this still counts as a missed reference, so make sure to include: a) quotes from reliable sources, b) in text citations (as appropriate), and c) your full reference list (at the end of your work/as footnotes or endnotes as per your reference system)

<u>A proper introduction</u> – Again, you'd be surprised how often people forget to properly introduce their work. Your written introduction can help HUGE amounts in setting out the criteria you wish to be marked against. If you introduce your research question or the issues you will discussing in a full, clear and concise manner, your examiner will have no choice but to mark against what you've set out to achieve. For instance: if you state in your introduction that you will be looking at a specific area of research **ex**cluding x, y and z, then the person examining your work cannot penalise you for not including those elements in your submission. On the other hand, if you don't make your research question explicitly clear, then you might find yourself with feedback that states: "the field of examination was quite narrow. Perhaps you could have included x, y, and z" BUT if this was never your intention, then say it from the off, so there is no confusion!

<u>Links to the industry</u> – This is particularly prevalent in postgraduate degrees, where you are assessed on whether your contribution to the existing field of study is unique. However, linking up with industry practice is still advisable and is a very positive addition to any papers submitted for an undergraduate degree. What I mean by this is mentioning how your studies relate to the current conventional practice within your industry and discussing what elements of your study you will take forward to apply to any future professional role. If you come across the work of a particular professional or practitioner that has changed the way you approach your profession, then make sure you state this (and reference where applicable) From this, you can suggest how the industry could adapt and evolve based on what you have uncovered, or indeed how your own professional practice has enhanced based on new or existing theory. As a lecturer and a working professional and academic, it is always so refreshing to read a student's perspective on how the industry is evolving and new techniques and schools of thought that are about to enter the workplace. Never underestimate the power of your submission to make substantial changes. As lecturers and professionals, we are always learning – and the sooner you start to view us as colleagues and fellow contributors to your chosen field of study, the more we can educate each other on how best to fulfil our roles.

FOR VIDEO SUBMISSION/ PRESENTATION/ PERFORMANCE EXAMS

<u>As before: A proper introduction</u> – Your introduction is where you're able to set out your research questions, and in the case of a physical exam, when you're able to showcase your personality and set the tone for success. At the risk of sounding a little bit patronising (apologies in advance), never underestimate the power of a polite and enthusiastic welcome. No matter how nervous you're feeling, if a candidate exudes charisma and confidence in the opening moments of any presentation or exam, I automatically enter the mind-set of "this person has prepared and knows exactly what they're talking about." It helps any examiner form a favourable opinion of the work you're about to present, before you've even begun to present it!

<u>A short context for each part of the submission</u> – Whether you're performing pieces of music for a recital or explaining the thought behind pieces of art of technology, you'd be amazed at the number of students who forget to explain the context or rationale relating to their particular submission. You'd have heard the analogy "pretend the examiner is an alien from outer space" all the way through school – but it very much applies here. I've examined many a singer who presents a truly beautiful performance, but forgets to tell me what their song (in Russian) is about – and given that I don't speak Russian, I'm therefore unable to give them an excellent interpretation mark, simply because I have no basis to mark their performance against! The same goes for portfolio or academic presentations: If you don't explain exactly what you set out to achieve, then you're throwing

away the opportunity to be marked fully against your own research questions. For instance, if you set out to create a piece of art that specifically aims to (let me think) make recycled rubbish look beautiful, but forget to state that this was your specific intention – then you leave yourself open to examiners questioning why you made your art out of rubbish, instead of out of canvas and paint. Does this make sense?

I know it seems totally obvious and something that probably goes without saying, but you'd be SO surprised by the number of students who lose out on substantial marks because they simply haven't set out what they aimed to achieve, and so the overall purpose and rationale behind their submission seems ambiguous or questionable.

<u>The opportunity to ask questions (if this is applicable and appropriate to your area of presentation)</u> – Whilst many presentation-based assignments have a question element or "viva voce" written into the mark scheme, there are some that don't. I've seen students celebrating the fact that they weren't asked any questions on their work and "got off lightly" with the content of their exam – however, this is not necessarily a good thing. While you might be thinking that not having to answer any questions is an easy way out, inviting the examiners to quiz you on your work can actually do you huge favours. If you know your subject inside out, upside down and round and round, wouldn't you want to have your knowledge challenged so you can prove just how expert you are?! Letting the examiners enquire as to your rationale and reasons for your particular choices or opinions is essentially another way of saying: "Is there anything that

wasn't clear that you're thinking of marking me down on? If so, can I clear this up for you now?" This is your chance to claw back any marks that may have been deducted through a lack of clarity — it's a unique opportunity to have an influence on your grade after your overall presentation or performance has finished.

BUT — the disclaimer here is: Honesty is the best policy.

If you find yourself having been asked a question that you have no idea what the answer is, sometimes it's just better to be honest about this. Frame your answer a bit like this: "That's a really interesting viewpoint that I hadn't thought of. I don't want to give you an answer that might be incorrect at this moment, but I'd happily follow this up with you once I've had a chance to evaluate your viewpoint in a bit more detail — or even simply: "I hadn't thought of that. I shall certainly look into it"

Obviously, there are some questions that you just should know the answers to, but if you do find yourself being asked something a bit outside of the study remit, I much prefer it when students respond with something like the above, rather than flailing around to give an incoherent and possibly incorrect answer. Examiners do sometimes like to ask you questions that might well be a bit outside of your research topic. Sometimes this is to test how far your knowledge extends, but most of the time it's because they are genuinely curious about your work and want to see how much knowledge you've already got covered!

Now, I'm going to say something here that might be a little controversial — but as honesty is a key theme of this book, I think it's important that I share my insights with you.

As a lecturer, I should probably be telling you that your final exams are the most important stage of your university journey — but in actual fact, I don't believe they are. Particularly in the case of the creative industries, but even in industries that are further afield, it often just doesn't seem right to reduce your entire university experience to one number. The fact of the matter is that what you have achieved by going to university and getting your degree is far more vast and expansive than what those final exam results represent. Many students spend so much time fretting and worrying about what their final classification is going to be, that they lose sight on what they have already actually achieved.

If you work hard, you will see results — this is proven. BUT, if you worry and stress, not only are you letting your final university moments pass you by, but you're also not putting yourself in the right headspace to achieve your very best when it really matters. I often spend a lot of time with my students, trying to ease their minds ahead of final exams when they've got themselves in a bit of a head spin — and it's always the case that those who approach the challenge with a sense of calm, fun and perspective do better in the end.

YOU are more than your mark. No matter what you get in your degree, if you go into an interview and exude your natural charm, charisma, intelligence and passion, the employer will want you on their team — regardless of whether your degree classification is first class or second class.

Don't get me wrong, this is by no means telling you that final exams don't matter — OF COURSE THEY DO...but they are not the be all and end all. And if you get the bug for education in the same way that I did, they will simply serve as your passport to your next stage of higher education.

Taking your final exams is a very exciting time for you! It's the time when you need to be enjoying your closing moments of your university experience and putting yourself in the best possible position for a successful career going forward.

Make the moments count — but make ALL the moments count.
You are more than a mark on a piece of paper.
You are unique!

GRADUATION: TIPS FOR GETTING THROUGH THOSE FINAL WEEKS OF STUDY & HOW TO PREPARE FOR AND ENJOY THE BIG DAY!

You've had this moment in the back of your mind when you submitted your first application. You visualised it so clearly when you walk the campus corridors on that very first enrolment day. Maybe this is something you've dreamed about ever since you were a young child. Well, the big moment is finally very near. You're just a few exams away from that cap and gown, that moment when you get to strut across that stage in front of your friends and family as they glow with pride. You've made it this far, and for that you deserve a maHOOSIVE pat on the back!

Getting through the last few weeks of study can be an exciting and challenging time. There's final exams and deadlines to think about, but from my university experience, I remember a distinct focus on trying to take everything in to make the memory last. I remember trying to map the corridors in my mind, and taking mental pictures of the usual seat I sat in for each particular class – little did I know that I would be back so soon (but that's beside the point!) From watching my own students walk the corridors for their final time before moving on to their own bright futures, I've realised that there are many tips I wish someone had given me for my closing university moments. I hope these little pieces of advice help you make the most of the end of your university journey:

Move your deadlines a week or two ahead of when they actually are

This is something I always liked to do as a student, and in fact I continue to do it in my professional career even now. What's often the case in your final semester of university study is that all of your deadlines come at once. This can be very stressful if there are many of them, and can take the enjoyment out of your final university moments. If you plan your submissions in an academic diary, then it can be useful to move your submission deadline a couple of weeks before the official one. This helps you make sure that your work is submitted on time and can help to stagger the workload so you have more free time to yourself.

Make the most of the ability to "resubmit" if you can

Many online submission tools (Turnitin being the most common) have a "resubmit" option available that can be implemented if your lecturer allows. What this enables you to do is submit your assessment, and then upload any amended versions in its place up to the point of the usual deadline. Whilst I'm by no means advising you to keep uploading half-finished drafts until you complete your final version, what I have seen some of my students do is upload a finished version that they're happy with well ahead of the deadline, and if they have any time free to enhance this even further later on, they can still continue to work on it. If, however, you're continually busy, then you have already submitted a very credible assessment and don't need to worry about rushing to complete it before the deadline arrives. The "resubmit" option is not available for all assessments, but it's worth checking whether this is an option for your modules to enable you to plan the spread of your workload accordingly.

Have a career talk with your personal tutor/relevant lecturers

If you're not intending on staying on for any further education, the final few weeks of university might be the last chance you get for a career talk with a knowledgeable person from your industry. If you're not yet set on the path you want to take or the options that are open to you, booking a meeting with your personal tutor or appropriate module lecturer is a great opportunity to get honest advice on where you will find most success in your chosen industry. Don't forget that most members of your module staff will have watched you grow and develop both academically and personally over the course of the past few years, and as such they will be able to give you the most trustworthy advice on how you are likely to achieve the most professional success.

Prioritise fun just as much as your studies

While so much of the uni experience centres around fun and independence, it is never more important than in your final few months of university to enjoy the ability to let your hair down. Before the responsibilities of work and money kick in fully, make sure you allow yourself time to relax and celebrate the end of an era, and a massive personal achievement. With good time management and strong preparation for approaching deadlines and final exams, there's no reason why you can't find plenty of time to go out and enjoy yourself. Make the most of being with the people on your course – as you all move back to your own parts of the world and take up work, it's unlikely that you'll all be in the same room together again (except for any future reunions that you might plan!) Take time to talk to you classmates, and keep in touch with them. You never know when your paths might cross again...you may just end up working alongside each other!

Then just like that, your lectures have finished, your assessments have been submitted, you've received your final marks through – and YOU'VE DONE IT!

The next big milestone in your university journey is of course...graduation!

Now, graduation day can be a very alien experience! Honestly, I've never experienced anything quite like it. The whole day went by in a flurry of nerves and excitement and concern that somehow, I was going to be the one person to get the whole thing wrong! Having attended a few graduations, let me give you a few top tips to hopefully ease any of these worries and allow you to enjoy your special day without any added stress!

Take note of your ceremony time
Whilst your university may only be running one graduation day, it is highly likely that that day will be divided up into a number of different ceremonies (usually grouped by your

"school" or discipline) Make sure you know which ceremony is yours! While getting there too early is never a bad thing, I'd hate to think of the alternative!

Remember to order/hire your gown in advance

Your university will let you know which robing company supplies your cap and gown (Ede and Ravenscroft is the most common one!) You will be able to hire or buy your cap and gown, in your particular size. I actually decided to buy mine — it was about £300 (so quite a big expense.) Little did I know that my sister would go on to study exactly the same degree as me, at exactly the same university — and conveniently enough, we are exactly the same size! (So, guess what she's wearing for graduation day! — nothing like getting your monies worth!) If you're planning on buying your cap and gown, make sure to remember to purchase the hood as well! (The hood is the coloured bit that goes over your black robe, and the colour scheme will be unique to your university) Be sure to get your order completed in good time, as it can take some weeks for it to be posted to your home address. If you're hiring your graduation robes, these will usually be delivered to your graduation venue along with all the other student's orders. When placing your hire order, you'll usually be given a reference number (sent by email), which you'll give to a member of staff when you arrive (though sometimes your surname is enough) You'll go through the process called "robing" where members of staff will be on hand to ensure that your graduation robes are on correctly (they can be surprisingly easy to get wrong) — and then you'll be good to go!

<u>Always assume that your head is bigger than it actually is!</u>
<u>(To save a head-crunching graduation cap!)</u>
If I'm brutally honest with myself, I wish I had ordered the next size up for my graduation cap! At the time, I didn't want to admit that I'd underestimated the size of my head by quite some way, so I put up with the feeling that my head was in a vice for two VERY long hours! Honestly, the way that mortarboard was perching on the top of my head, I may as well have stuck a propeller on the top and made it a piece of novelty headgear! So, in short – it doesn't hurt to add on an extra half an inch to your head measurement...you'll thank me for it later!

<u>Remember to get your application in for any extra tickets</u>
<u>ASAP</u>
Whilst I can't guarantee that this will be the case for your particular university, it is not unheard of that you may have the opportunity to apply for an extra ticket(s) to the graduation ceremony. Every student will be guaranteed two or three (for parents/other family members), and whilst I appreciate you may want your whole family to attend your special day, unfortunately if every student did this, they'd never fit everyone in! However, not every student uses up their guaranteed tickets, and as such, any spares go into a pot where others can apply for extra. This is usually on a first come, first served basis, and your university will advise if there are any spots for the taking. Be sure to get in quick, and keep in mind that there are no guarantees – but it's worth a shot!

<u>Don't wear shoes you can't walk in!</u>

The highlight of your graduation ceremony is that walk across the stage. I'm sure you've all had nightmares about face planting in front of everyone – but let's not do anything that enables these horror dreams to become reality! Whilst I'm neither a fashion expert (you won't need to look far to find someone to agree with this!) or a nagging mother, I can't tell you how much better you'll feel for choosing shoes that are comfortable more than daring! Trust me, I've been there. I went to a wedding once, and I wore these most amazing red shoes that I absolutely adored. They didn't have my size in the shop, so I had to buy them one size bigger – and bloody hell! You know when you have to clench all of your toes at once in a bid to try and manually grip the shoes to your feet – well, that's what I spent about eight long hours doing. I'd practically dropped another shoe sizer by the end of the day from the amount of toe-clenching I had to do! So, whenever I see graduating students hobbling across the stage in the way I am all too familiar with, I feel more upset for them than I am excited to be sharing their special moment with them – and whilst you may be feeling physically uncomfortable, you don't want your audience to be feeling uncomfortable for you! Take my advice on board here – I speak from experience!

<u>Safety pins are your best friend!</u>
Ladies and Gents, it never hurts to have a safety pin or two in your pocket on graduation day. Trust me when I say, those hoods NEVER fit properly – and if you look back at your graduation pictures and realise that your hood is hanging down round your ankles, you'll want to kick yourself! It's best to fasten the hood at the shoulders, with a pin on each side – this should avoid any problems later!

Don't have any belongings on you that can't be put in a pocket!

This is yet another thing I learnt the hard way! I remember keeping my phone and asthma inhaler to hand (as I usually do) during the ceremony, but it wasn't until we were called to line up ready for our procession that I realised I had no pockets to put them in! We were told prior to the start of the ceremony that we may not end up in the same seats we started in, so I couldn't leave them on my chair. What I ended up doing was asking the guy next to me who I very vaguely knew (Mark I think his name was), to put my phone and inhaler in his pockets. Luckily, he found the whole thing very funny, but facing the prospect of having to juggle shaking the vice chancellor's hand with my hands full was a very nerve-wracking couple of minutes! The best thing to do is leave all your belongings with your family and arrange a place to meet in the venue after the ceremony has finished to save you needing your phone.

Get someone else to take responsibility for picture-taking

This is a day you're going to want to look back on for many years to come, and the best way to do that is of course through pictures. Amidst the chaos and stress of remembering to be in the right place at the right time, the last thing you need is to be worrying about taking pictures. More recently, I've heard of students asking a particular family member or friend to take responsibility for taking the photographs on the day – this can avoid everyone either worrying about pictures and taking many of poor quality, or assuming somebody else has taken on the job and then forgetting to take any at all. If somebody in your graduation party has photography skills and a good camera (though a phone will more than suffice these days!) then it can be a weight off your mind to ask them to play the photographer. You'll have much less stress and worry, better pictures, and all the photos in one place to make sharing much easier. If you're not planning on any further education, this will be your first and last graduation ceremony, so it's important to capture the very special moment as best you can!

Don't be alarmed when the 'scroll' is fake!
You'll all be aware of the famous graduation shot, with the graduate wearing their cap and gown and holding the "degree scroll." On the day of my graduation, I was very alarmed to realise that this "scroll" doesn't really exist! If you pay for professional pictures (which can usually be booked and paid for on the day), you'll most likely be given a plastic scroll to hold for the purposes of the famous picture, but you won't actually receive anything on the day! Usually your official degree certificate comes in the post ahead of the ceremony. Don't be shocked to go away without an official document...chances are, you've already received it!

Lastly, there remains little for me to say except...ENJOY IT. Raise a glass to your wonderful achievement. Cheers to you!

YOUR PROFESSIONAL "PACKAGE"

If you've followed the steps of my previous chapters, then you might have already prepared your appropriate documents ready to present at interviews to potential employers. If you never got round to it, not to worry! I'll recap everything you might need to prepare here, so you can secure that interview for that dream job — and hopefully succeed in getting it!

Your CV

This one goes without saying, and I cannot overstate how important it is to get right. Whilst your CV can be largely the same for every job you apply for, it's worth remembering that it can be changed and adapted to better suit any prospective position. For instance, if you're applying for a customer service/client liaison based role, you might like to stress your communication skills and ability to work effectively both in a team and as an individual. If, however, your role is not client-facing and perhaps more knowledge and research based, you might want to consider focusing in on your motivation, work-ethic and ability to work effectively under pressure and to deadlines, alongside your excellent knowledge of the industry. While your listed qualifications, awards and experience will remain the same, it's worth going over your first introductory "personal statement" to choose the adjectives that most fit the role you are applying for. It really does make all the difference.

A covering letter

This will typically be sent in alongside your CV to any organisation you are applying for a role within. When writing my own covering letters and helping my students to do the same, I find it helps to think of it like a personal introduction to the formal CV. Whilst, as in your CV, your broad content will remain the same, your covering letter is the perfect chance to exhibit just how much you want to work in that particular role, in that particular company. Always remember to mention the company name, the role you're applying for, and if possible try to state a reason why you chose them to apply to. Perhaps they are one of the leading names in your chosen industry. Or maybe you're personally familiar with their work?

Try a format like this (and fill in the blanks/amend where appropriate!):

Dear Sirs,

My name is <u>NAME HERE,</u> and I'm writing to you to apply for the role of <u>JOB TITLE</u> within <u>COMPANY NAME</u>. As one of the leading businesses in the industry, I would very much like to be a part of your continuing development in <u>A PARTICULAR FIELD</u>.

After this, you can state a bit more about yourself:

I am a recent graduate of <u>UNIVERSITY,</u> where I achieved:

Then state some of your notable achievements whilst studying.

Outside of university, I also:

Then state some of your notable achievements outside of university.

I would relish the opportunity to bring my knowledge and enthusiasm to your company and I thank you for your time in considering my application.

Please don't hesitate to contact me, should you wish to discuss my application further.

Think of your covering letter as a highlights reel. State your best, most impressive bits alongside your passion for working within the company – then let your CV do the talking when it comes to the full range of your abilities (and I'm sure it's very expansive!)

Portfolio pictures where applicable

Of course, the requirements of this will differ greatly depending on what your field of study is. For artists and designers, I'm sure the portfolio element of your professional package will go without saying. Actors and performers should/will have a portfolio of pictures ("headshots") to be sent to casting directors with a view to being asked to audition for a particular role. However, even if none of this applies to your field of study and the industry you're going to enter, you might like to consider whether a professional "headshot" would be a positive addition to your CV or any other materials you are looking to submit alongside your application?!

Last but by no means least, make sure that you use the letters after your name that you have earned from achieving your degree. I see so many people neglecting to use their academic letters, but they're a sign of all of your hard work! Make sure you use them and be proud — they signify a great achievement!

MAKE AN IMPACT THAT EXTENDS FURTHER THAN YOUR STUDIES

By the time this part of the book matches up with where you are in your higher education journey, you may already have settled into your first job as a graduate – or perhaps you're not quite there yet. Regardless of how far you've walked down your particular chosen path, whether you're reading this book ahead of your first university semester, or whether you've already received your first salary payslip, you will have something in common – and that is a passion and enthusiasm for your chosen subject. In the crazy haze of university, it's so easy to lose sight of why you enrolled in the first place, and whilst your reasons for doing this may be different to other people's, we have all chosen the subjects we did for the same reason – we loved them.

If you haven't already, you will eventually settle into your employment – and whilst you may find that your job is more interesting and rewarding than you ever could have imagined, never lose sight of your personal value. Going to university will not only have taught you the fundamental knowledge of your particular profession, but over the course of your studies, you will have also got to know your own strengths and weaknesses and what unique contribution you as an individual are able to bring to your particular field. Once you're wrapped up in the responsibilities of your job, it can be easy to become distracted away from making this unique contribution – but I'm here to tell you that your industry relies on it!

The world is a crazy place, and is changing at a faster rate than ever before. So many industries are having to find ways to adapt and evolve in order to continue being able to meet the needs and expectations of the modern consumer. My particular specialism is opera, and I'm sure you can imagine how many problems this industry is facing with falling audience numbers and a lack of engagement in younger generations. My PhD research aims to provide possible solutions to this issue by suggesting how the industry as a whole is able to modify – but I'm sure that opera is not the only field facing similar issues. Having only just graduated from university, you have all of the most current knowledge and your whole career ahead of you in order to explore and expand this. At this point in time, you have a unique opportunity to make lasting change to your chosen profession, and you mustn't lose sight of this.

Your university goal lists are often the lists that are the most honest and optimistic lists you'll ever write – and it's for this reason that you mustn't throw them away. The ambitions written down on these lists were written at a time when perhaps you didn't yet have the knowledge to put these plans into action, but you did have the enthusiasm and motivation...now, you have all that knowledge – so try to hold on to that enthusiasm!

Getting your degree is a wonderful achievement, and will probably be up there with the most satisfying and rewarding moments of your life – but it's only the start of your journey!

If you're reading this book at the beginning of your studies, try to hold on to this thought, and let your passion and enthusiasm see you through to achieving success — and if you're reading it in "real time", and are already in/searching for employment, let this serve as a reminder of what you have already achieved. You are skilled, determined and remarkable — and your journey has only just begun.

GLOSSARY

Lots of study-specific terms are covered throughout this book in their appropriate chapters, however, I thought I'd pick out a few terms and definitions that might be worth repeating! Of course, if you're looking for something specific, you might find it easier to flick back to the appropriate chapter and find what you're looking for in context – but here are a few of the more frequently used terms, and a bit about what they mean:

Assignment: Any piece of work given to you as part of your studies. Remember that sometimes assignments form part of your assessments, and the two words are sometimes used interchangeably.

Alumni: Somebody who has completed a university course becomes part of the university alumni. Most universities offer alumni schemes such as continued library access or use of resources.

Bachelor's/Bachelor's degree: An undergraduate degree that is usually awarded after three or four years of study.

Blackboard: An online platform specific to your university, where you are able to submit work, view announcements, watch back video lectures etc. (The most common alternatives to this are Moodle or Brightspace, but the functionality is the same)

Campus: A university premises. Remember that a university may have multiple campus sites.

Clearing: A period of time before the start of the new academic year that matches prospective university students to the remaining places available in universities across the country. Most universities have a clearing hotline that enable you to contact them direct. However, you can typically search universities with clearing places available through UCAS.

Conditional offer: An offer from a university that depends on you meeting certain conditions (most commonly specific grades in your A-level exams.)

Course leader: A member of staff in charge of a whole course, who also oversees all of the modules under the course umbrella. They may or may not teach on any of the modules, and hole more of a managerial role, in charge of the course as a whole.

Defer/deferral: Putting off your studies for a period of time (usually a year). You can defer your studies in the middle of your degree to take a year out, though universities can differ in their process for arranging this.

Foundation year: A foundation year is an extra year's study before the start of a university degree course. It's usually for students who haven't quite met the required standard for entry onto the normal course to bridge the gaps in their knowledge before embarking upon their studies for a full degree.

Levels: At university, you may hear the terms 'level 4, level 5, level 6 and level 7' Level 4 students are students in their first year, level 5 is for second year students etc. Level 7 is for postgraduate students (usually studying for master's degrees)

Master's/Master's degree: A degree awarded by a university after one or two years further study, following the completion of a bachelor's degree. (In the same, or a closely related subject)

Mitigation: You can apply for mitigation which can enable extra time to complete an assessment or more lenient marking if your personal circumstances have meant that you are unable to follow the usual submission process. You will typically need to provide evidence of such circumstances before mitigation can be granted.

Module: Essentially a class. A module will have a title and will focus on a particular area of study. Each module will have its own assignments and exams.

Module leader: A member of staff in charge of a particular module. They usually instruct module tutors on the content to be delivered, and typically report to the course leader who oversees the course that their particular module is a part of.

Module tutor: A member of staff who teachers a particular module. They report to the module leader, and follow the curriculum set out by them.

Personal tutor: A common feature of most universities, a personal tutor is a member of staff responsible for the welfare and development of a particular year group or group of students. You would typically bring any academic or personal problems that impact your university studies to your personal tutor who will be able to help and advise you.

Postgraduate: A student at university who has already completed and achieved their first degree, and who has progressed onto further higher-level degree study.

Remediation: If you don't meet the required standard to pass a module, some universities offer a period of remediation, where you are able to resubmit the work during the remediation period (usually between 3-6 months) prior to your removal from the course.

Semester: A half-year term usually used especially in universities. Each year will usually have two semesters and these will usually last around fifteen weeks. However, some universities divide their year up into three chunks (just like the autumn, spring and summer terms at school)

Student finance: Regulated and run by the student loans company, all eligible students will be entitled to tuition fee loans and maintenance loans where applicable. Tuition fee loans will be paid direct to your university by the student loans company, and maintenance loans will be paid direct to you. You will only start repaying your student loan when you earn above the repayment threshold.

Student services: Whilst the name may differ between universities, all institutions will have an onsite team to assist in everyday matters ranging from finance to personal wellbeing. Your student services team should be your first point of call for any issues you face, and if they cannot resolve it, they will refer you to the appropriate person or department.

Student union: Every university will have a student union, which is a support team (that will be largely student or alumni-run) to look after your needs. The student union can provide academic and personal support as well as plenty of fun, recreational
activities. They are there to work for and support you, above all else! There is no requirement to "join" You are already a member just by being a student.

UCAS: Stands for University and College Admission Services. UCAS is an admission channel through which applications can be made to most universities. Most university applications will be made through the UCAS website.

Unconditional offer: An offer from a university that does not on you meeting certain conditions. No matter what results you receive in your A-level exams, this offer will still stand.

Undergraduate: A student at university who hasn't yet completed their first full degree course (which is usually a bachelor's)

Withdrawal: A notice that a student no longer wishes to continue on their chosen course at university.

Madeline Castrey is a musician, performer and educator from Surrey, England.

She was the first 16-year-old admitted onto a degree course at The London College of Music and graduated with a Master's degree in 2017. After graduating, Madeline was invited to take on a lecturing role within the institution, becoming one of the youngest lecturers in the country. She has also built an established performance career, having appeared in several West End, television and London opera productions.

Madeline is also the proud recipient of a Princess Diana Award for fundraising, having raised huge amounts for various national and international causes. One of her main ambitions is to improve accessibility to music, and as such, Madeline has pioneered the formation of several projects and organisations to provide new ways to engage with music and the arts. She has composed two charity singles featured on radio and television shows alike, and has many future ideas in the pipeline!

madelinecastrey.co.uk

Instagram/Twitter: @madelinecastrey

www.blossomspringpublishing.com

Printed in Great Britain
by Amazon